AN ALTERNATE REALITY

See From Heaven's Perspective And Manifest Heaven On Earth

CHAD GONZALES

AN ALTERNATE REALITY

REALITY

See From Heaven's Perspective
And Manifest Heaven On Earth

CHAD GONZALES

An Alternate Reality: See From Heaven's Perspective And Manifest Heaven On Earth

ISBN: 978-1-7354232-4-1 paperback
ISBN: 978-1-7354232-5-8 hardback
Copyright © 2021 by Chad W. Gonzales
Chad Gonzales Ministries
www.ChadGonzales.com

TABLE OF CONTENTS

INTRODUCTION

In 1999, an American science fiction movie was released by Warner Brothers called *The Matrix*. The movie depicts a dystopian future in which humanity is unknowingly trapped inside a simulated reality called "The Matrix." There is a powerful scene in which the two main characters, Neo and Morpheus, have a conversation in which Morpheus explains the Matrix and gives Neo an opportunity to see beyond the simulated reality.

MORPHEUS   Welcome, Neo.   As you no doubt have guessed, I am Morpheus.

NEO It's an honor to meet you.

MORPHEUS The honor is mine. Please, come. Sit. I imagine that right now you're feeling a bit like Alice...tumbling down the rabbit hole?

NEO You could say that.

MORPHEUS I can see it in your eyes. You have the look of a man who accepts what he sees...because he's expecting to wake up; ironically, this is not far from the truth. Do you believe in fate, Neo?

NEO No.

MORPHEUS Why not?

NEO I don't like the idea that I'm not in control of my life.

MORPHEUS I know exactly what you mean. Let me tell you why you're here: you know something. What you know, you can't explain, but you feel it. You felt it your entire life. Something's wrong with the world. You don't know what, but it's there...like a splinter in your mind...driving you mad. It is this feeling that has brought you to me. Do you know what I'm talking about?

NEO The Matrix?

MORPHEUS Do you want to know...what it is? The Matrix is everywhere; it is all around us...even now, in this very room. You can see it when you look out your window or when you turn on your television. You can feel it when you go to work...when you go to church. . . .when you pay your taxes. It is the world that has been pulled over your eyes...to blind you from the truth.

NEO What truth?

MORPHEUS That you are a slave. Like everyone else, you were born into bondage...born into a prison that you cannot smell or taste or touch. A prison....for your mind. Unfortunately, no one can be told what the Matrix is. You have to see it for yourself. This is your last chance. After this, there is no turning back. You take the blue pill...the story ends, you wake up in your bed and believe whatever you want to believe. You take the red pill, you stay in Wonderland and I show you how deep the rabbit hole goes. Remember, all I'm offering is the truth.

What Neo discovers is an alternate reality, which in fact, is the true reality. Although *The Matrix* was a fictional story, there is a tremendous truth that is applicable in our real world. Most Christians do not realize it, but there are two realities we are dealing with in our everyday life on the Earth. There is the reality of this world and an alternate reality. The world's reality is based on the curse on the Earth; this reality has been the reality for almost all of mankind since the Garden of Eden. Every once in a while, a man or woman would operate in this alternate reality and as a result, those around them would experience the supernatural power of God. Those under the Old Covenant such as Moses, Joshua, Elijah and Elisha tapped into this alternate reality; however, it wasn't until Jesus Christ provided redemption that it became available for every one of us to make a choice between "the red pill and the blue pill."

As we go through this book, you'll begin to discover a world that many of us have dreamt about or thought was only for the "Bible days." You will find that God has left up to you and I how far we want to go in living according to this alternate reality while on the Earth.

This book is an endeavor to show you what is available, to show you how far we have sold ourselves short and yet how we can raise our standard of life to that of Jesus Christ Himself. We are going to discover how we can renew our mind, change our perspective, and set ourselves apart so that we can manifest the world we are from in the world we live in. Keep reading and you will discover an alternate reality which you can live in starting right now.

1

A TALE OF TWO REALITIES

After the Lord's supper, Jesus prays in the upper room as He prepares for His arrest and crucifixion. This time of prayer is the only time recorded in the Gospels in which we truly get to hear Jesus' words to the Father. It is one of my favorite passages of Scripture because Jesus makes so many wonderful statements of truth regarding the purpose of His coming, our union with the Father and our purpose on the Earth. We also find a powerful truth Jesus speaks of that, rarely, if ever, gets spoken of from our Christian pulpits: an alternative reality.

John 17:13-19 NKJV
13 But now I come to You, and these things I speak in the world, that they may have My joy fulfilled in themselves. 14 I have given them Your word; and the world has hated them because they are not of the world, just as I am not of the world. 15 I do not pray that You should take them out of the world, but that You should keep them from the evil one. 16 They are not of the world, just as I am not of the world. 17 Sanctify them by Your truth. Your word is truth. 18 As You sent Me into the world, I also have sent

them into the world. 19 And for their sakes I sanctify Myself, that they also may be sanctified by the truth.

Notice Jesus states that He is not of this world. Jesus was in all respects an alien; He was born in Heaven, sent from Heaven and sent into this Earth to do a job and then return back to Heaven. This was very much a consciousness of Jesus in that He was sent from another world. Throughout the book of John, Jesus refers to being "sent by the Father" forty one times; this was a major part of Jesus' success on the Earth and in manifesting the supernatural.

Jesus then goes on to pray for His disciples (which includes you and I, as Jesus mentions this in verse 20). Jesus states that His disciples are not of this world in the same way He is not of this world. (For an in depth study on this subject, please refer to my book *Aliens*.)

Now let's take a look at verse 17.

John 17:17 NKJV
Sanctify them by Your truth. Your word is truth.

In this short statement lies a hidden yet powerful revelation for us in which Jesus' entire prayer is wrapped around. The word *sanctify* is the Greek word *hagiazo* which means *to consecrate, separate or purify.* So Jesus' prayer is for the Father to separate them by His truth.

Now this is where things get interesting. Most people would read over this and simply take this statement that when we live by the words of God, it will help us to live separate and pure lives that will distinguish us from the sinner. Although it is true that living according to God's commands will help us live holy lives, this statement Jesus makes is not about that - it is way more than that!

The word *truth* here is the Greek word *aletheia* and can simply be defined as *reality*. Essentially, Jesus says, "Father, separate them from the world by your reality. Your Word is reality." Now, look at this closely. Jesus is talking about another reality here, an alternate reality - something different than what everyone else is experiencing.

Jesus gives us a major clue as to why He was getting supernatural results. How was He walking on water, calming storms, turning water into wine, multiplying food, raising the dead and healing the sick? It wasn't because He was Jesus. Yes, Jesus was the son of God, but He laid aside all of those advantages and lived, prayed, ministered, and healed as a man anointed by God.

> Philippians 2:5-8 NKJV
> 5 Let this mind be in you which was also in Christ Jesus, 6 who, being in the form of God, did not consider it robbery to be equal with God, 7 but made Himself of no reputation, taking the form of a bondservant, and coming in the likeness of men. 8 And being found in appearance as a man, He humbled Himself and became obedient to the point of death, even the death of the cross.

Jesus was living life as a man, anointed by God but living according to another reality. He wasn't living according to the reality of this world with its impossibilities; Jesus was living in an alternate reality while on the Earth. It was Jesus desire that His disciples (which includes you and I) would live permanently in this alternate reality as well while on the Earth.

Now let's think about this. Jesus' time with the disciples was not to simply make them good, moral, well behaved men. Jesus' time with the disciples was to make them representatives of Heaven with power and authority exactly as Jesus had while on the Earth. Jesus then states in verse 19 that He separated Himself by Heaven's reality so that the disciples could also be separate on the Earth by that same reality.

It was Jesus' desire and purpose for the disciples to replicate Him with perfection so that even when Jesus was no longer on the Earth, the same ministry of power would continue through all those who became united with Him through salvation.

So what is this alternate reality? It is a reality in which the Life of God rules; it was the reality God gave to Adam in the Garden of Eden.

> Genesis 2:26-27 NKJV
> 26 Then God said, "Let Us make man in Our image, according to Our likeness; let them have dominion over the fish of the sea, over the birds of the air, and over the cattle, over all the earth and over every creeping thing that creeps on the earth." 27 So God created man in His own image; in the image of God He created him; male and female He created them. 28 Then God blessed them, and God said to them, "Be fruitful and multiply; fill the earth and subdue it; have dominion over the fish of the sea, over the birds of the air, and over every living thing that moves on the earth."

Before Adam sinned, Adam had complete dominion over the Earth and everything in it; there was nothing that was not under his control. He not only had control over the animals but Adam also had control over the earth. The water, the ground...all of it was under his authority. Look at what people like Moses, Joshua, Elijah, Elisha and Jesus did with nature; if they could accomplish that after the curse, *imagine what Adam was able to do before the curse!*

Adam was living in the Blessing. The kingdom of God was in complete dominion. There was no sickness, no death, no lack and unhindered access to Heaven because there was no sin.

> *Sin and the sense realm would now rule mankind.*

However, the moment Adam sinned, everything changed. What was his reality changed. His physical senses began to slowly become the leader of his life and his spiritual sensitivity began to slowly fade away. Sin had taken over and Adam accepted it. Sin and the sense realm would now rule mankind.

There was now a new reality for Adam - a reality dominated by the curse. In Genesis 3, God tells Adam about the results of his choice and the reality that would now be his.

FROM A WATCHMAN TO A WORKER

Genesis 3:17-19 NKJV
17 Then to Adam He said, "Because you have heeded the voice of your wife, and have eaten from the tree of which I commanded you, saying, 'You shall not eat of it':"Cursed is the ground for your sake; in toil you shall eat of it All the days of your life. 18 Both thorns and thistles it shall bring forth for you, and you shall eat the

herb of the field. 19 In the sweat of your face you shall eat bread till you return to the ground,For out of it you were taken; for dust you are, and to dust you shall return."

It was now a life that would be ruled by death. Adam went from being a guardian to a gardener. *His sole job in the Garden of Eden was to guard and protect what was provided to him; now Adam would have to work for everything he needed.*

Adam traded a weapon for a shovel and went from being a watchman to a worker. In the Garden, everything Adam needed for life was already provided. It was a life of grace and he traded it for a life of works in a reality ruled by the curse.

All living things would now began to decay. The life of God that was in mankind to protect it from all sickness, disease, pain and decay was now gone. Man was left to his own understanding and ways to walk according to the world of death. Access to Heaven was shut. Sickness and disease would reign supreme. Flu season and allergy season would become just as normal as fall, spring, summer and winter. Doctors would eventually take the place of God as the source of healing and the love of many would begin to grow cold. This is what would now become the reality of the world: a life of limitations, death, destruction, famine, poverty, disease and dependence on self.

THE CURSE HAS BECOME NORMAL

The world's reality is what is normal for us because it is what we have grown up in. From the time you arrive in this world, we become indoctrinated by society that getting a cold is normal. If you get a fever or sore throat during the winter season, it is normal. If you get a headache or muscle aches, the solution is to take some aspirin or other over the counter medications.

The world's reality tells us that if someone is diagnosed with cancer, the only "real" solution is to undergo chemotherapy and/or radiation. This reality looks at doctors as the sole source of physical help. The reality of the curse is that as you grow older, you get weaker in your mind and body. The world's reality is that if you are born with a genetic disease, it is just your lot in life. *The world's reality is simply this: what you see is what you are stuck with.*

You are told all of these things as you grow up from your family, teachers, church, media and society. Sickness, lack, impossibilities... they are everywhere you go! It is the world's reality.

As a result, what used to be normal in the Garden of Eden would now become a life of faith for those who would pursue it and yet, those who did would be few and far between. The reality of Heaven would now become an alternate reality and the reality of a cursed filled and dominated world would now become the reality of mankind.

There would be a few throughout the thousands of years until Jesus that would catch a glimpse of this alternate reality and for brief moments, access it and manifest Heaven. They would raise the dead, divide waters, heal the sick, stop the sun - the stories of some of the Old Testament saints sometimes read like a superhero story.

Some would say it was because they were special; no, it was because they lived according to this alternate reality. It may have sometimes been for days at a time and sometimes just for a few minutes, but every time they did, the supernatural became natural and the impossible became possible in that moment.

HEAVEN'S REALITY

We could use many words and phrases to describe this alternate reality. It's a reality of life, truth, and blessing as opposed to the world's reality of death, lies and the curse. It is the reality of Heaven on the earth. It is the kingdom of God versus the kingdom of Satan; the kingdom of light versus the kingdom of darkness. For the sake of ease and consistency, we will refer to it as Heaven's reality. It is Heaven's reality that can be tapped into and lived from all while living in the world.

> 1 Corinthians 6:11-13 MSG
> 11-13 Dear, dear Corinthians, I can't tell you how much I long for you to enter this wide-open, spacious life. We didn't fence you in. The smallness you feel comes from within you. Your lives aren't small, but you're living them in a small way. I'm speaking as plainly as I can and with great affection. Open up your lives. Live openly and expansively!

The cry of God for His creation is to live this wide open, spacious life, free of the limitations of this cursed reality. There is a reason that innately, we identify with superheroes and constantly look for ways to go beyond the limitations we experience with our senses. Instinctively, we know there should be more but can't see it because of the dullness of our hearts. Even the sinner, the person far from God still recognizes there is more to this life. Built into our being is an innate desire to push the limits and boundaries of what we experience with our senses. Why? Because God originally created us to dominate the world with all power and authority.

While others are living according to the world's reality of death and decay, we can live in the world's reality and yet live according to an alternate reality; a reality that supersedes that which most of humanity knows. The ability to look at death and yet see life; to look at a mountain and see it as a molehill; to look at a live cancer and yet see it as dead.

It was this alternate reality that Jesus came to not only introduce, but also make possible for us to live in, live from and manifest while alive on the Earth.

2

I AM REALITY

There are many Scriptural reasons we see as to why Jesus came to the Earth. Yes, we know Jesus came to save us but He also came to do several other things: one of them being to show us what was possible as a man or woman filled and united with God. Jesus was not only revealing the Father but also revealing what was possible when we saw and thought like the Father.

In John 14:6, Jesus makes a statement that is very familiar but has been glossed over. He says, "I am the way, the truth and the life." We understand Jesus is the only way to the Father; as much as that is coming under attack in our current society, there is no other way to the Father but by Jesus!

After declaring that He is the way, He declares that He is the truth. Now here is where it gets interesting. The word *truth* in the Greek literally means *reality*. In other words, not only were the words and actions of Jesus the truth but they were also reality. Jesus was revealing an alternate reality that was full of life. Jesus was letting them know He was the way to the reality of God's life!

When Jesus was in the Garden of Gethsemane and the soldiers asked if He was Jesus of Nazareth, Jesus' response was "I Am." It wasn't just an answer to their question but an acknowledgment, manifestation and demonstration of this alternate reality; *it was an invasion of the kingdom of Heaven into the cursed world in that very situation.*

> ## *Jesus was endeavoring to show His disciples how to live as a son of the Blessing as opposed to a son of the curse.*

Jesus' ministry was not just bringing salvation and revealing the love of the Father, but it was also combating the impossibilities of the physical realm and showing another world from which to live. Jesus was endeavoring to show His disciples how to live as a son of the Blessing as opposed to a son of the curse. This is why when Jesus sent the disciples out to preach and heal the sick, it was to be a manifestation of the kingdom of God; the alternate realities of Heaven usurping the realities of the cursed world.

> Luke 9:8-11 NKJV
> 8 Whatever city you enter, and they receive you, eat such things as are set before you. 9 And heal the sick there, and say to them, 'The kingdom of God has come near to you.' 10 But whatever city you enter, and they do not receive you, go out into its streets and say, 11 'The very dust of your city which clings to us we wipe off against you. Nevertheless know this, that the kingdom of God has come near you.'

Notice that the sick being healed was an experience of the kingdom of God; the righteousness of God overriding the unrighteousness of the world. It was the experience of an alternate reality; a reality greater than what we experience with our physical senses.

For those who refused to receive the message of the kingdom of God, they were told the opportunity had been there to experience it, but because by choice, they had missed it. An alternate reality was available, but by their very own choosing, they continued to live according to this world's reality.

In John 3, Jesus and Nicodemus have a conversation about salvation; but it is much more than salvation. We view John 3:16 as the ultimate salvation scripture but in this entire conversation, Jesus is talking to Nicodemus about this alternate reality. Let's begin with John 3:3.

> John 3:4-16 NKJV
> 4 Nicodemus said to Him, "How can a man be born when he is old? Can he enter a second time into his mother's womb and be born?" 5 Jesus answered, "Most assuredly, I say to you, unless one is born of water and the Spirit, he cannot enter the kingdom of God. 6 That which is born of the flesh is flesh, and that which is born of the Spirit is spirit. 7 Do not marvel that I said to you, 'You must be born again.' 8 The wind blows where it wishes, and you hear the sound of it, but cannot tell where it comes from and where it goes. So is everyone who is born of the Spirit." 9 Nicodemus answered and said to Him, "How can these things be?" 10 Jesus answered and said to him, "Are you the teacher of Israel, and do not know these things? 11 Most assuredly, I say to you, We speak what We know and testify what We have seen, and you do not

receive Our witness. 12 If I have told you earthly things and you do not believe, how will you believe if I tell you heavenly things? 13 No one has ascended to heaven but He who came down from heaven, that is, the Son of Man who is in heaven. 14 And as Moses lifted up the serpent in the wilderness, even so must the Son of Man be lifted up, 15 that whoever believes in Him should not perish but have eternal life. 16 For God so loved the world that He gave His only begotten Son, that whoever believes in Him should not perish but have everlasting life.

Jesus told Nicodemus, "Most assuredly, I say to you, unless one is born again, he cannot see the kingdom of God." Not only was Jesus the way to the Father, He was also the way to living in this alternate reality. It is a reality full of truth and full of life; a reality in which righteousness prevails and Heaven is manifest on the Earth!

Jesus was telling Nicodemus not only how to be born again, but also how to live from another reality. Notice in verse 6-8, Jesus differentiates between those born of flesh and those born of the spirit or you could say those living according to the world's reality and those living according to Heaven's reality.

John 3:6-8 NKJV
6 That which is born of the flesh is flesh, and that which is born of the Spirit is spirit. 7 Do not marvel that I said to you, 'You must be born again.' 8 The wind blows where it wishes, and you hear the sound of it, but cannot tell where it comes from and where it goes. So is everyone who is born of the Spirit."

Again, two realities: flesh and spirit; the world's reality and Heaven's reality. Jesus compares Heaven's reality to the wind; you

24

may not see where it comes from, but you will definitely experience its impact in this physical realm.

THE SON OF MAN WHO IS IN HEAVEN

Where the conversation gets really interesting is in verse 12 and 13. Jesus says, "If I have told you earthly things and you do not believe, how will you believe if I tell you heavenly things? No one has ascended to Heaven but He who came down from Heaven, that is, the Son of Man who is in Heaven."

In the midst of this conversation, Jesus continues to compare the reality of the world and the reality of Heaven. After being shocked that Nicodemus, being a religious teacher and leader did not understand these things, Jesus drops a bombshell of a statement. *Jesus says, "Not only did I come from Heaven, I'm in Heaven right now."*

> *You can live in this world, but live from another world and experience a different result.*

Can you imagine the look on Nicodemus' face? He must have initially thought Jesus had lost His mind! Here was Jesus physically standing in front of Nicodemus and Jesus says, "I am in Heaven." What was Jesus talking about? Jesus was letting Nicodemus in on a secret: you can live in this world, but live from another world and experience a different result.

If you want to see Heaven's reality, simply look at Jesus; He showed us what the will of God was on the Earth. Jesus showed us what was possible as a man or woman filled with God and united with God.

I am thankful for the powerful men and women of God who have come before us as examples to follow; however, *Jesus is my standard.* It is Jesus whom I will always measure everything up to and determine what should be in my life and how I should handle it.

Jesus showed us what was possible as a man living on the Earth but living from Heaven; however, if we are to do the works of Jesus, we must share the same perspective He had while on the earth.

3

RESCUED AND REMOVED

When we are born into this world, we are here like everyone else living in a cursed world - a world dominated and ruled by disease, poverty, death and impossibilities; a world where we are left to fend for ourselves. All those who have not received Jesus as their Lord and Savior are under the rule of Satan, blinded from the truth and imprisoned by the darkness.

When we receive Jesus as our Savior, thank God, things change for the son of God! God takes us out of the kingdom of darkness and places us into the kingdom of light.

Colossians 1:12-14 TPT
12 Your hearts can soar with joyful gratitude when you think of how God made you worthy to receive the glorious inheritance freely given to us by living in the light. 13 He has rescued us completely from the tyrannical rule of darkness and has translated us into the kingdom realm of his beloved Son. 14 For in the Son all our sins are canceled and we have the release of redemption through

his very blood.

Even though physically you are in the same place after salvation, spiritually things changed; suddenly, you began to contact two different worlds. Because of your union with Christ, you now can live from Heaven's reality while walking through the world's reality.

SAVED AND SENT

You were translated into God's kingdom! The Church, the new creation is literally an invasion into the sense realm. You see, we have gotten it backwards; we are looking at ourselves as earthlings trying to get Heaven to invade Earth - but we are seeing it all wrong. We are the sent ones! We are the invaders.

We see ourselves as saved, but not sent; therefore, we look out from Earth instead of looking into Earth. We are looking at Heaven from the outside in and it must be reversed. Just as with Jesus, when we were born again, we were born from Heaven and sent from Heaven to invade the Earth; to live among the world's reality while manifesting Heaven's reality. Friend, we were saved!

SAVED FROM THE CURSE

Have you ever thought about it? When you were saved, what were you saved from? You were saved from the curse. This is why the word *salvation* in the Greek is so powerful. The Greek word for *salvation* is *soteria* and means *preservation, deliverance, safety and health; the deliverance from the molestation of enemies;the deliverance from all earthly ills.*

28

When you say, "I am saved" you are literally saying, "I've been delivered from all earthly ills." You are also saying, "I am healed!"

It's important for us to see that when we were saved, *we were rescued completely!* Completely! This means Satan has no power over you. This is what it means to be redeemed!

Ephesians 1:7 NKJV
In Him we have redemption through His blood, the forgiveness of sins, according to the riches of His grace.

We hear the word *redemption* and sing about being redeemed but again, do we really believe it? The word *redemption* is the Greek word *exagoridzo* which means a *permanent removal from captivity.* In Bible days, this is what happened when a slave was purchased and then set free. Not only was the fee paid, but then the slave was released and removed completely from slavery; he was no longer a slave but a free man! The slave had been redeemed.

Jesus' death was not only the payment for our freedom but also the permanent removal of us from the situation. Redemption took us out of Satan's kingdom with the rule of the curse and transferred us into God's kingdom with the rule of life!

Sickness and disease have no more power over you. We were absolutely removed from the tyrannical rule of darkness and placed into Heaven's reality. Spiritually, we changed kingdoms and a new way of living was made available to us. How is that possible? Because the sin that held us in bondage and tied to the curse was canceled out. We were declared righteous in God's sight and therefore qualified to partake of everything Heaven had to offer.

Galatians 3:13 TPT
Yet, Christ paid the full price to set us free from the curse of the law. He absorbed it completely as he became a curse in our place. For it is written: "Everyone who is hung upon a tree is doubly cursed."

All that we were before Christ was tied to the curse. When we were born again, we were literally born again and set free! The old us died and a new man became alive. The man who was tied to the curse died and a new man was born into God's kingdom, thus having access to live from Heaven's reality while living in the Earthly world. Redemption put you in a position where you can literally say, "I'm from Heaven, going to Heaven and yet living from Heaven right now!"

4

SATAN REALLY IS DEFEATED

It is imperative we understand our position in Heaven's reality versus Satan's position in the world's reality. Before salvation, we were under the rule and influence of Satan.

> Ephesians 2:1-3 NKJV
> 1 And you He made alive, who were dead in trespasses and sins, 2 in which you once walked according to the course of this world, according to the prince of the power of the air, the spirit who now works in the sons of disobedience, 3 among whom also we all once conducted ourselves in the lusts of our flesh, fulfilling the desires of the flesh and of the mind, and were by nature children of wrath, just as the others.

The apostle Paul refers to Satan as "the prince of the power of the air who works in the sons of disobedience." I am not denying Satan's rightful, albeit stolen position, in the world; however, for the child of God, things changed for us on the day of salvation. Before salvation, Satan was in control of us; after salvation, we are in control of him. Before salvation, we were a child of the curse; now we are a child of the King!

The sad thing about this fact is that most Christians do not understand redemption - that we were redeemed from Satan's authority.

> Colossians 2:12-15 TPT
> 12 For we've been buried with him into his death. Our "baptism into death" also means we were raised with him when we believed in God's resurrection power, the power that raised him from death's realm. 13 This "realm of death" describes our former state, for we were held in sin's grasp. But now, we've been resurrected out of that "realm of death" never to return, for we are forever alive and forgiven of all our sins! 14 He canceled out every legal violation we had on our record and the old arrest warrant that stood to indict us. He erased it all—our sins, our stained soul—he deleted it all and they cannot be retrieved! Everything we once were in Adam has been placed onto his cross and nailed permanently there as a public display of cancellation. 15 Then Jesus made a public spectacle of all the powers and principalities of darkness, stripping away from them every weapon and all their spiritual authority and power to accuse us. And by the power of the cross, Jesus led them around as prisoners in a procession of triumph. He was not their prisoner; they were his!

Everything that tied us to this cursed reality was obliterated because of Jesus. He then stripped Satan of his authority and power over us and then had a victory parade!

I love the Passion translation of verse 13. Notice he refers to the world's reality as "the realm of death" because that is exactly what it is; the world's reality is a curse filled, death-dominated reality. Jesus removed us from that and put us into Heaven's reality or you could say the realm of life!

Friend, Satan really is defeated! Because of this removal, Satan literally has no authority over you - none! Jesus stripped him of his authority over us; how much more clearer does it get?

Matthew 28:18 NLT
Jesus came and told his disciples, "I have been given all authority in heaven and on earth.

SATAN NEEDS YOUR AUTHORITY

If Jesus has all authority, that means someone has no authority. Do you get it? Satan has no authority over you. This is why he goes about looking for who he can devour; he is looking for Christians who don't know their rights and privileges in Christ. Satan can't make you sick and he can't kill you; Satan can't kill, steal and destroy unless we allow him too. In other words, because Satan has no authority, he is looking for your authority. *He needs your authority to operate in your life.* I know that statement isn't popular but it is what it is: truth.

We have given Satan too much credibility in the life of the Christian. Yes, he has a pseudo rule in the world because people continue to allow it but in Heaven's reality, Satan has nothing. Although we may have to currently live in this world's reality, we don't live from it; we live from Heaven's reality that usurps the world's reality. In the reality from which we live, Satan is a non issue as long as we don't give him a place.

Does this mean that Satan won't try to bring harm your way? By all means no! Satan is a liar, a deceiver, a tempter and he hates you. He would like nothing more than to see you get so consumed with things in this death realm, you become a non factor for him. Satan wants to destroy you, but he can't unless we allow it.

When we come to the realization that Satan truly is defeated, it will change our perspective and our response in dealing with his threats and challenges. It is the reason Jesus would stand before a demon and emphatically demand the demon leave.

> *Jesus still remembers the day He stripped Satan of his authority over us and stood there as The Eternal Champion.*

Jesus was always operating from the standpoint of the victor, never the defeated trying to get the victory.

If we are going to operate in this alternate reality, our mind must be renewed to the undisputed fact that Satan is really defeated. If we continue to look to the sense realm for what is real, it may seem that Satan is in full control. We can look at the millions of people who are dealing with sickness, poverty and a host of other issues and think that Satan is in control; yet, we must make sure we are viewing life through the perspective of Heaven.

Heaven knows and sees Satan is defeated. Jesus still remembers the day He stripped Satan of his authority over us and stood there as

The Eternal Champion. Jesus knows beyond any shadow of doubt that Satan is defeated; the question remains, "Do we know?"

Many of the absolutes of which we are to live by in this alternate reality hinges on this basic but powerful truth: Satan is defeated. If Satan is defeated, then everything that is produced by him is already defeated and will stay that way unless we give him authority - then it will defeat us.

Knowing this allows you stand before all of the products of this world's reality, this death realm, and rebuke it in your life. This absolute allows you to stand before the storms of life and command them to stop, to curse a disease and command it to go or to refuse the poverty that has run through your family for generations.

Friend, Satan really is defeated!

5

DEAD MEN WALKING

Because we died with Christ, we are no longer subject to the curse; we have been set free! The problem that we face though is that most Christians do not realize it. Yes, we may quote it, sing it and declare it, but we must face fact: most of us do not believe it.

We must begin to see things the way Jesus sees things. We must go beyond head knowledge and move into reality.

> Romans 6:1-4 NKJV
> 1 What shall we say then? Shall we continue in sin that grace may abound? 2 Certainly not! How shall we who died to sin live any longer in it? 3 Or do you not know that as many of us as were baptized into Christ Jesus were baptized into His death? 4 Therefore we were buried with Him through baptism into death, that just as Christ was raised from the dead by the glory of the Father, even so we also should walk in newness of life.

Notice the apostle Paul says that because we died with Christ, we also should walk in a new type of life. In other words, the same life Jesus lives right now, is the very same life we are to live right now. I know that sounds like a crazy statement but it is right there in your Bible.

THE ONLY DIFFERENCE
BETWEEN YOU AND JESUS

You must understand the only difference between Jesus and you right now is your body. He has a heavenly body and you have an earthly body; however, it reveals that we can experience just as much of Heaven on Earth in an earthly body as with a heavenly body. Think on that!

> Romans 6:5-7 NKJV
> 5 For if we have been united together in the likeness of His death, certainly we also shall be in the likeness of His resurrection, 6 knowing this, that our old man was crucified with Him, that the body of sin might be done away with, that we should no longer be slaves of sin. 7 For he who has died has been freed from sin.

Remember that sin was the foundation for all of the world's problems. Sin was the lifeblood of the curse; when Adam sinned in the Garden of Eden, the curse overtook the earth. Sin was the thing that tied me to that curse; but when I received salvation, I died and a new Chad was born. As a result of what happened, I am now alive unto God but dead unto the world.

THE THREEFOLD NATURE OF THE CURSE

The curse was basically three fold: spiritual death, sickness and poverty (Deuteronomy 28); therefore, when we see the word *sin*, we can interchange any of these three areas and not add or take away from the Scripture. You could read Romans 6:7 like this: "For he who has died has been freed from sickness."

Now I know many Christians would look at that and say, "Well, if I am free from sickness, then how come I'm still dealing with sickness?" *The answer is simple: you still believe you are alive unto it.*

We need to change our perspective on sickness and poverty. I know some religious folks get up in arms about it, but they can stay sick and poor if they want. I choose to be healthy and wealthy because that is what Jesus provided.

DEAD TO SICKNESS

In this area of sickness, we must see ourselves as dead to it. Have you ever seen a dead person get sick? Obviously, we know dead people can not get sick because they are dead! You will never see a prayer chain of healing started for people that are dead because they are no longer susceptible to sickness and disease.

Well, if you are dead to sickness, that means you are a dead person walking in this Earth in which no disease can touch you. This is why we should not be afraid of any sickness or disease in this Earth! Disease no longer has any power over me. Disease no longer has any authority over me. Because I am alive unto God and dead to the curse, I am no longer susceptible to any disease that is around me. No plague or calamity come against my body! A thousand may fall at one side and ten thousand at another, but it can't come on me!

I know the majority of people hear me talk like that and think I've lost my mind; they are right. I'm not thinking like a cursed man anymore; I'm thinking like a blessed man now! People living in the world's reality see themselves susceptible to the diseases of this world; people living in Heaven's reality see themselves immune from the diseases of this world. How could I get sick when I am dead to sickness?

When I was forgiven, that is when I was healed. When Jesus removed the sin problem, He removed the sickness problem too. When the sin was removed from me, the sickness was removed from me. The cursed, sick, broke Chad died and the blessed, healed and rich Chad was born.

BLESSED BUT LIVING CURSED

Now, if I don't see according to Heaven's reality, I will see myself as going to Heaven one day but still living with the world's problems. *If I don't see according to Heaven's perspective, I will see my spirit alive unto God, but my body still alive unto sickness; I will live blessed in my spirit but cursed in my body.*

> Romans 6:10-14 NKJV
> 10 For the death that He died, He died to sin once for all; but the life that He lives, He lives to God. 11 Likewise you also, reckon yourselves to be dead indeed to sin, but alive to God in Christ Jesus our Lord. 12 Therefore do not let sin reign in your mortal body, that you should obey it in its lusts. 13 And do not present your members as instruments of unrighteousness to sin, but present

yourselves to God as being alive from the dead, and your members as instruments of righteousness to God. 14 For sin shall not have dominion over you, for you are not under law but under grace.

Reckon yourself to be dead to sickness. The word *reckon* simply means *to consider to be true*. You don't need to consider something to be true that is obvious to your senses. I guarantee that you have never looked in the mirror and wondered if you were an elephant. Why? Because everything in this sense realm reveals you are a human being. Now if you wanted to believe you were an elephant, it would take some serious considering wouldn't it? It sounds funny but that is actually what is going on today.

More and more we are seeing boys allowing their minds to run wild and considering themselves to be a girl and vice versa. After a while of doing lots of considering, they see themselves to be the opposite sex even though they are not. We know these things to be true in the natural world; at some point, we must realize it is true in the spiritual world as well.

> *We must stop looking to the sense realm to tell us what is reality.*

In this world, we live by our senses and allow our senses to show us what is reality. This is the reason hundreds of millions of God loving Christians suffer with sickness and disease. Even though we are saved and delivered from disease, we still look to the physical sense realm to tell us what is reality regarding sickness and our bodies. As a result of looking and considering the sickness, we continue to get sick because that is what becomes reality to us.

41

What you put your focus on is what you become the most aware of; what you are aware of is what you will believe. We must stop looking to the sense realm to tell us what is true. The sense realm is dominated by the curse; therefore, it is impossible for you to see what is true.

This is why Paul tells us to consider ourselves to be dead to sin and sickness but alive unto God. You can't be alive to God and alive to sin and sickness but you can be alive to God and still ruled by sin and sickness.

Everything in this world shouts that you are alive to sin. This is why the vast majority of churches preach so much on sin - because even the pastor doesn't realize they are free from sin!

Everything in the world also shouts that you are alive to sickness. This is why we are inundated with television commercials and social media ads about cancer, viruses and medications. The world's reality is telling everyone, "You are under the dominion of sickness" but the Holy Spirit is yelling "No you are not!"

> Romans 6:23 NKJV
> For the wages of sin is death, but the gift of God is eternal life in Christ Jesus our Lord.

So many people quote Romans 6:23 in regards to people's sinful ways but Romans 6:23 isn't about sin; it is about righteousness. When you keep it in context to what Paul is teaching us in Romans 6, verse 23 should make you shout! The result of the curse is death, but the gift of righteousness gave us life! Not just life when you die physically and go to Heaven, but victory over darkness right now!

The life of God is a possession you have right now which allows you to be free of all sickness and all disease. You aren't waiting for Heaven to experience eternal life; you can experience it right now and enjoy it right now. The only hindrance - and I truly mean the only hindrance - is your perspective. *Your problem is not the devil; your problem is your perspective.*

> *I must make a decision that I will not be a redeemed person living a cursed life.*

You must see yourself exactly the way Jesus saw Himself on the earth: dead to the curse in this world. What you see will determine what you experience. I must make a decision that I will not be a redeemed person living a cursed life; I see myself alive unto God and dead to sickness. Say it with me, "Sickness has no dominion over me; I'll never be sick another day in my life because I am redeemed!"

6

REPENT

After Jesus left the wilderness from being tempted for forty days by Satan, the Bible says Jesus began to preach and say, "Repent, for the kingdom of heaven is at hand."

Most often, when we hear the word *repent*, we think of sorrow. We picture those times when we did something wrong and felt horrible for it; however, feelings of remorse for past actions are very different from Biblical repentance.

The Greek word for *remorse* in the New Testament is *metamelomai* and expresses grief, sorrow and regret. *Metamelomai* is the word used that described the guilt Judas experienced after he betrayed Jesus. You could say that remorse is more of an emotional response to one's actions.

In contrast, the Greek word for *repent* is *metanoeo* which means "to change one's mind." This is a complete change of one's mind and ways; a decision to completely turn around one's thinking, believing or living.

The Greek scholar Rick Renner said this about the word repent:

> The Greek word *metanoeo* is a compound of the words meta and nous. The word *meta* in this context refers to a turn or a change. The word *nous* is the word for the mind, intellect, will, frame of thinking, opinion, or a general view of life. When the words *meta* and *nous* are compounded in the word *repent*, it portrays a decision to completely change the way one thinks, lives or behaves. *Metanoeo* reflects a turn, a change, a change of direction, a new course and a completely altered view of life and behavior. (*Sparkling Gems From the Greek 2*, page 277-278).

As we can see from this definition, repentance is not just accepting a new belief, perspective or idea; repentance is a radical conversion to a truth that causes a complete change in perspective, thinking and living.

Jesus began His ministry by saying, "Change the way you see, think and live because the kingdom of Heaven is here!" Jesus was letting them know there was a new way of seeing and living; there was an alternate reality available for them to access!

The kingdom of Heaven was not an earthly kingdom. The Jews were expecting the Messiah to become their earthly king, bring about an earthly rule, and defeat all those who were ruling over the Jews - but this was not what Jesus was preaching. Jesus was declaring that Heaven's reality was now available for anyone who wanted it.

Mark 6:1-13 NKJV

1 Then He went out from there and came to His own country, and His disciples followed Him. 2 And when the Sabbath had come, He began to teach in the synagogue. And many hearing Him were astonished, saying, "Where did this Man get these things? And what wisdom is this which is given to Him, that such mighty works are performed by His hands! 3 Is this not the carpenter, the Son of Mary, and brother of James, Joses, Judas, and Simon? And are not His sisters here with us?" And they were offended at Him. 4 But Jesus said to them, "A prophet is not without honor except in his own country, among his own relatives, and in his own house." 5 Now He could do no mighty work there, except that He laid His hands on a few sick people and healed them. 6 And He marveled because of their unbelief. Then He went about the villages in a circuit, teaching. 7 And He called the twelve to Himself, and began to send them out two by two, and gave them power over unclean spirits. 8 He commanded them to take nothing for the journey except a staff--no bag, no bread, no copper in their money belts-- 9 but to wear sandals, and not to put on two tunics. 10 Also He said to them, "In whatever place you enter a house, stay there till you depart from that place. 11 And whoever will not receive you nor hear you, when you depart from there, shake off the dust under your feet as a testimony against them. Assuredly, I say to you, it will be more tolerable for Sodom and Gomorrah in the day of judgment than for that city!" 12 So they went out and preached that people should repent. 13 And they cast out many demons, and anointed with oil many who were sick, and healed them.

Notice when Jesus encountered all of the unbelief, He began

teaching in all of the villages. What do you think He was saying? "Repent, for the kingdom of Heaven is at hand!" Heaven's reality was the major focus of Jesus ministry! Jesus was trying to tell people about a new way of living, but they were so ingrained in this cursed reality and so offended at Jesus because of their familiarity with Him, there was no repentance. So what was Jesus solution? Keep teaching; keep giving them truth in order for them to renew their mind to this new reality.

After Jesus commissioned the twelve disciples, He sent them out to do the same thing He was doing.

> Mark 6:12-13 NKJV
> 12 So they went out and preached that people should repent. 13 And they cast out many demons, and anointed with oil many who were sick, and healed them.

The disciples went out to tell people, "Change your perspective on life!" and then gave them the proof of this alternate reality, Heaven's reality, by casting out demons and healing the sick.

STOP GOING THE DIRECTION OF DARKNESS

Jesus wanted people to stop going the direction of the kingdom of darkness, the cursed world's way of doing things, and go the direction of the kingdom of God. This is why healing was such a tremendous part of Jesus ministry. Not only did Jesus want people free of their pain and discomfort, but He wanted them to see natural proof of a supernatural reality. *It was an invasion of a world they could not see into a world they could see!*

When Jesus sent out the seventy disciples, Jesus said, "Heal the sick and tell them the kingdom of God has come near to you." Up until that point, the people had to depend on doctors and the crazy spiritual beliefs and customs that had been brought in by the Romans and other kingdoms that had ruled the Jewish people. The people had to rely on the world's way of doing things to hopefully get rid of their problems. Now mind you that disease, at its root, is a spiritual problem. You can't deal with spiritual issues with natural solutions!

Jesus was healing people according to Heaven's way. Jesus was showing that Heaven's reality was the answer to the world's limitations in every arena of life. People were stuck in a cursed reality and didn't even realize that the life they were experiencing was not the will of God.

Can you imagine being the lepers and outcasts in that society - forbidden to be around people and live outside of the city walls? Imagine when you do get the opportunity to be in the vicinity of people, you have to yell "Unclean!" so that people do not get too close to you.

YOU MUST BE WILLING TO DIE

Friend, that isn't life! So what was Jesus answer? Repent! Change your perspective. Turn your back on your old way of living. Die to the cursed way of living. Die to the life that is sense ruled and come alive to the world that is spirit ruled. To live in this alternate reality would require a dying to self; a life that's dominated by self, dependent on self and looking to self for every resource.

This is why Jesus told the disciples, "For whoever desires to save his life will lose it, but whoever loses his life for My sake will find it" (Matthew 16:25). Do you want true life? Do you want life the way God desires for you to have? Then you have to die to your current way of living.

It will require a complete 180 degree turn. It will be a life that is lived by faith in a world you can't see with your senses so that it can manifest in the world you can see with your senses.

> 2 Corinthians 5:6-7 NKJV
> 6 So we are always confident, knowing that while we are at home in the body we are absent from the Lord. 7 For we walk by faith, not by sight.

We most often associate this passage of Scripture with physical death, but there is also the powerful truth here of "dying to our self." *The less aware you are of yourself, the more aware you are of the Lord* or you could say the less confident/aware you are of this natural world, the more confident and aware you are of the spiritual world.

Repentance is choosing to die to your self.

Repentance is choosing to die and it's not a one time death, but a continual choice. There will always be opportunities to die to self, die to the old way of thinking, and die to the old perspective. We should gladly choose repentance each and every time.

THE PERSPECTIVE OF
THE PHARISEES AND HEROD

Jesus had a tremendous job on his hands in helping the disciples understand this alternate reality and the renewing of mind it would take. When this cursed reality is all you know and you experience it twenty four hours a day - it will take a great deal of work by the Holy Spirit and your cooperation to change your perspective.

Mark 8:15 NKJV
Then He charged them, saying, "Take heed, beware of the leaven of the Pharisees and the leaven of Herod.

After Jesus had just multiplied food and fed the four thousand, He and the disciples got into a boat to head over to Bethsaida. Jesus then warns them about the leaven of the Pharisees and Herod. Jesus wasn't talking about real leaven but the perspective of the Pharisees and Herod.

The Pharisees were the religious leaders of the society and were very educated and very intellectual. They knew the Old Testament forwards and backwards but had no revelation. Their biggest issue was they were full of information, but no revelation. They were sticklers for the Scripture but had no belief in the supernatural. Jesus never condemned their knowledge of Scripture but He did condemn their hardness of heart and unbelief of the supernatural things of God.

On the other hand, Herod's perspective on life was simple: he was his own god. If Herod needed something, he was his provider.

Both of these perspectives are the way people live in a cursed reality: we are our source and the answers are always in this physical realm.

This was Jesus' warning to the disciples: do not live like this and always be on guard of this type of thinking because it will rob you. What was the answer? Repent! Repent of thinking you are the answer for your problems. Repent for thinking the answer is always here in the physical cursed world. Die to that way of thinking and live according to Heaven's reality.

This reality would allow them to rise above the limitations of this world and access the realities of Heaven; however, in order to access it, it would require repentance from their former way of living and thus require a complete change of perspective.

7

A DIFFERENT PERSPECTIVE

There should be a difference in the marriages, finances, health and overall life of the Christian compared to the sinner. When Jesus prayed, "Father, set them apart by Your reality" Jesus was letting us know what He knew...there was an alternative reality for the one united to God.

Don't you think the life and results of one united to God should be far greater than the person united to Satan? Absolutely! The problem is that, although we were given access, if you don't know it is available, you can't access it - this is where most Christians are at.

When we received salvation, our old man died and we became a brand new creature in Christ (2 Corinthians 5:17). Once we were saved and united with God through Jesus Christ, this alternative reality, Heaven's reality, became available for us to live in.

Colossians 3:1-4 NKJV
1 If then you were raised with Christ, seek those things which are above, where Christ is, sitting at the right hand of God. 2 Set your mind on things above, not on things on the earth. 3 For you died, and your life is hidden with Christ in God. 4 When Christ who is our life appears, then you also will appear with Him in glory.

The majority of Christians get saved and think their Christianity is about a change in morals and behaviors, but don't realize it is to also result in a change of reality. Our spirit sees and hears clearly; it is our soul that must be transformed. *We are to begin seeing differently so that even though we are in the same situation as the sinner, we get different results;* we get supernatural results because we are operating according to Heaven's reality.

Romans 12:2 MSG
Don't become so well-adjusted to your culture that you fit into it without even thinking. Instead, fix your attention on God. You'll be changed from the inside out. Readily recognize what he wants from you, and quickly respond to it. Unlike the culture around you, always dragging you down to its level of immaturity, God brings the best out of you, develops well-formed maturity in you.

There is a reason the apostle Paul spent so much time talking to the Christians about renewing their mind and changing the way they saw things. It is because when you are born in this world, you are born into a world that lives according to the curse. People on the Earth think that results of the curse are a normal way of living. They may not realize that death, sickness, disease, lack, poverty, etc is the result of the curse; however, they are familiar with the results of the curse and assume it is just part of life.

CURSED THINKING

When we are saved but continue to think like the world, we will still get the limitations of the world and results of the world. You can be saved and still have cursed results because of cursed thinking. This is what Paul was referring to in Romans 12:2 The world is always dragging you down to its level but God's way will lift you up and break the barriers off of your life.

> 2 Corinthians 6:11-13 MSG
> 11-13 Dear, dear Corinthians, I can't tell you how much I long for you to enter this wide-open, spacious life. We didn't fence you in. The smallness you feel comes from within you. Your lives aren't small, but you're living them in a small way. I'm speaking as plainly as I can and with great affection. Open up your lives. Live openly and expansively!

When my first response to sickness is the same as the sinner...I still have cursed thinking and it must be renewed so my life can be transformed. When I think like the world, it is because I am carnally minded; I am sense ruled. If your mind isn't renewed, you can have the power of Heaven in your spirit but be dominated by a defeated enemy.

You can be saved and still have cursed results because of cursed thinking.

Romans 8:5-6 NKJV
5 For those who live according to the flesh set their minds on the things of the flesh, but those who live according to the Spirit, the things of the Spirit. 6 For to be carnally minded is death, but to be spiritually minded is life and peace.

When you live a life with your mind on the ways of this world, you will get worldly results, even though you are seated with Christ in heavenly places and all the resources of Heaven are yours. It's actually sad to think about it! It's like someone living on the streets, hungry and homeless, yet they have one million dollars in their bank account. It doesn't make sense does it? You would think, "Who in their right mind would live like that?"

> *The person filled with God should have it better than the person filled with the devil.*

Sadly, about 99.9 % of Christians live their lives this way every day: rich but living poor; healed but living sick.

WHAT IS NORMAL?

We are taught growing up that it is normal for people to get sick - it is just part of life. We are taught it is normal that as you age, you get weaker and begin to lose your mind - it is just part of life. Now for the sinner, the curse is their reality; for the Christian, it is supposed to be different. The person that is filled with God should have it better than the person who is filled with the devil!

Colossians 3:1-4 MSG
1-2 So if you're serious about living this new resurrection life with Christ, act like it. Pursue the things over which

Christ presides. Don't shuffle along, eyes to the ground, absorbed with the things right in front of you. Look up, and be alert to what is going on around Christ—that's where the action is. See things from his perspective.
3-4 Your old life is dead. Your new life, which is your real life—even though invisible to spectators—is with Christ in God. He is your life. When Christ (your real life, remember) shows up again on this earth, you'll show up, too—the real you, the glorious you. Meanwhile, be content with obscurity, like Christ.

Our old life is dead; therefore, our way of living and our way of seeing should change! How does it change? By renewing our mind! We need to see things from His perspective; we must see things according to Heaven's reality.

COME UP AND LOOK DOWN

I'll never forget one time in which Lacy and I were dealing with a severe financial deficit at our church. Things in the natural did not look good at all and I had begun to get in fear about the situation. I was sitting on our back porch one day and just spending some time watching the sunset and praying in the spirit. All of a sudden, I heard these words, "Come up to where I am and see things from My perspective."

I closed my eyes and began to imagine myself seated at His side and looking down on my problems. Suddenly, those problems seemed small and I got joy and peace about the situation. It wasn't too long after that, a financial miracle happened and the dire situation was resolved. My problem was that I was looking at the situation from the standpoint of the world and not from the standpoint of

Heaven! It's no different than when you are on a plane. The things that look so big while you are on the ground become so much smaller when you get up 30,000 feet in the air. Your perspective changes everything!

INDEPENDENT OF CIRCUMSTANCES

Even under the Old Covenant, God had made provision for the Israelites to live independent of their circumstances. God was trying to show them what was possible living according to His reality. When you look at Moses and the Israelites, it is a powerful reminder of what God wants to do for us. When the plagues were being released on the Egyptians, did you ever notice the plagues never affected the Israelites?

> Exodus 8:20-24 NLT
> 20 Then the LORD told Moses, "Get up early in the morning and stand in Pharaoh's way as he goes down to the river. Say to him, 'This is what the LORD says: Let my people go, so they can worship me. 21 If you refuse, then I will send swarms of flies on you, your officials, your people, and all the houses. The Egyptian homes will be filled with flies, and the ground will be covered with them. 22 But this time I will spare the region of Goshen, where my people live. No flies will be found there. Then you will know that I am the LORD and that I am present even in the heart of your land. 23 I will make a clear distinction between my people and your people. This miraculous sign will happen tomorrow.'" 24 And the LORD did just as he had said. A thick swarm of flies filled Pharaoh's palace and the houses of his officials. The whole land of Egypt was thrown into chaos by the flies.

Even in the midst of a pandemic, what affected the Egyptians didn't affect the Israelites! I absolutely love what God says in verse 23: "I will make a clear distinction between My people and your people! That is the God we serve!

Exodus 9:4 NLT
But the Lord will again make a distinction between the livestock of the Israelites and that of the Egyptians. Not a single one of Israel's animals will die!

Exodus 9:26 NLT
The only place without hail was the region of Goshen, where the people of Israel lived.

Exodus 10:21-23 NLT
21 Then the Lord said to Moses, "Lift your hand toward heaven, and the land of Egypt will be covered with a darkness so thick you can feel it." 22 So Moses lifted his hand to the sky, and a deep darkness covered the entire land of Egypt for three days. 23 During all that time the people could not see each other, and no one moved. But there was light as usual where the people of Israel lived.

Exodus 11:7 NLT
But among the Israelites it will be so peaceful that not even a dog will bark. Then you will know that the Lord makes a distinction between the Egyptians and the Israelites.

DISTINGUISHED PEOPLE

There should be a distinction between God's people and the rest of the world. God wants you to be distinguished!

1 Peter 2:9 TPT
But you are God's chosen treasure—priests who are kings, a spiritual "nation" set apart as God's devoted ones. He called you out of darkness to experience his marvelous light, and now he claims you as his very own. He did this so that you would broadcast his glorious wonders throughout the world.

1 Peter 2:9 KJV
But ye are a chosen generation, a royal priesthood, an holy nation, a peculiar people; that ye should shew forth the praises of him who hath called you out of darkness into his marvellous light;

We were bought with a price and made to be God's chosen people. Just as the Israelites were God's natural nation, the Church is His spiritual nation. We are to be set apart from the rest of the world. We are to be a peculiar people! Have you ever seen someone that was peculiar? What made them peculiar? It was that they looked, dressed and/or acted different; there was something about them that made them stand out from the rest. This is the way God designed for us to live! God called us out of the darkness so we could broadcast the light!

> *You were bought by God to be peculiar and broadcast the light!*

Even though Heaven's reality should be our reality, if we do not change the way we think and begin to see like Jesus, we will not experience the results of Jesus. Remember: it requires repentance! The purpose of repentance is to shift you back from the world's reality to Heaven's reality.

I've said it for many years: "If you are going to do what Jesus did, you must think like Jesus thought." What you see will determine what you believe which will determine your results in life.

THE PERSPECTIVE OF JESUS

It is obvious that Jesus saw things differently. Jesus' perspective was far different than those around Him; consequently, Jesus experienced supernatural results in situations that looked impossible to the natural bystander.

In Jesus' mission of revealing the Father, Jesus was also revealing what was possible in this alternate reality. Many people want to attribute Jesus' supernatural results to the fact that He was God on the Earth. Although He was God on the Earth, the Bible is very clear that Jesus was operating on the Earth as a man.

Philippians 2:5-7 NLT
5 You must have the same attitude that Christ Jesus had.6 Though he was God, he did not think of equality with God as something to cling to. 7 Instead, he gave up his divine privileges;he took the humble position of a slave and was born as a human being.

It's important to always remember that Jesus, although God, was doing life as a man with a physical body and brain like you and I. As a result, even Jesus had to renew His mind. Yes, you read that right: *Jesus had to renew His mind.*

Jesus, although righteous in spirit, was being brought up in a world where sickness was normal and not everyone in Jewish society was living according to the law. In Jesus day, it had been a very long time since there had been a true prophet of God around who was working miracles. For many Jews, some of these true stories had turned into fables and for others, they were celebrated stories of the great days of God in the past.

Jesus said in John 5:20, "The Father will show me even greater things than these, just so you can marvel." In this statement, we see that (1) Jesus didn't know everything and (2) God was leading Jesus down a path of discovering what was possible in the reality of God. As God would show Jesus, it was a renewing of His mind taking place so that He could prove out the will of God.

> Romans 12:2 NKJV
> And do not be conformed to this world, but be transformed
> by the renewing of your mind, that you may prove what
> is that good and acceptable and perfect will of God.

Again, remember that to prove the will of God, our mind must be renewed in that area. You must be dead to the old way of seeing and open to the new way of living; dead to the curse and alive to the blessing.

We can't manifest what we can't see - and I'm not talking about our physical eyes. You must be able to see it in your soul and when you can, the will of Heaven is now ready to be manifest in the Earth. For God's perfect will to be manifest, we must see how He sees so we can do what He wants done.

THE PROGRESSION OF JESUS

In Jesus' life, there are two specific areas in which we see Him progress throughout the Gospels: dealing with water and dealing with death. In regards to water, the first miracle He performed was turning water into wine. Secondly, Jesus calms the seas and ultimately, Jesus walks on the water. There was a progression of dominance here but the progression began in His mind first. *As His mind was renewed to what was possible, He was able to prove out what was possible.*

In the area of death, we see this same progression. The first person we are told that Jesus raised from the dead was Jairus' daughter who had been dead a few hours. The second person we are told of that Jesus raised from the dead was the widow woman's son who had been dead for approximately one day. The third person we see Jesus raise from the dead was Lazarus who had been dead for four days!

Do you see the progression? *Every step of dominance was the result of an increased change of perspective.* Every demonstration of His authority was an ascent over the other - this was revealing that in the soul of Jesus, there was an ever ascending growth into God. His awareness of His authority and dominion over the world was continually increasing.

JESUS WAS INSPIRED BY OTHERS

I think sometimes we forget that Jesus had read the Old Testament. As a young Jewish boy, He would have read the stories of Moses, Joshua, Elijah, Elisha and many others who were used by God in the miraculous. In His reading, Jesus obviously didn't allow these stories to simply be stories; these stories served as not only inspiration but also a catalyst of miracles in His own life.

For instance, look at Elijah and Elisha. In looking at the miracles of Jesus, it's obvious Jesus took note of what happened in their lives.

In 2 Kings 4, we read of the Shunammite woman whose son had died. She went to Elisha for help and notice his response.

> 2 Kings 4:32-37 NKJV
> 32 When Elisha came into the house, there was the child, lying dead on his bed. 33 He went in therefore, shut the door behind the two of them, and prayed to the Lord. 34 And he went up and lay on the child, and put his mouth on his mouth, his eyes on his eyes, and his hands on his hands; and he stretched himself out on the child, and the flesh of the child became warm. 35 He returned and walked back and forth in the house, and again went up and stretched himself out on him; then the child sneezed seven times, and the child opened his eyes. 36 And he called Gehazi and said, "Call this Shunammite woman." So he called her. And when she came in to him, he said, "Pick up your son." 37 So she went in, fell at his feet, and bowed to the ground; then she picked up her son and went out.

Notice that Elisha shuts everyone out and goes in himself to the dead child; ultimately, the child is raised from the dead. Remember when Jesus raised Jairus' daughter from the dead? Jesus kicked everyone out of the house except for Peter, James, John, and the girl's parents; Jesus went into the dead child's room and raised the her from the dead.

After Elisha raised the Shunammite son from the dead, we read of another miracle which also was an inspiration for Jesus: Elisha and the multiplication of food.

> 2 Kings 4:42-44 NKJV
> 42 Then a man came from Baal Shalisha, and brought the man of God bread of the firstfruits, twenty loaves of barley bread, and newly ripened grain in his knapsack. And he said, "Give it to the people, that they may eat."43 But his servant said, "What? Shall I set this before one hundred men?"He said again, "Give it to the people, that they may eat; for thus says the Lord: 'They shall eat and have some left over.' " 44 So he set it before them; and they ate and had some left over, according to the word of the Lord.

For me, this is probably the most obvious of inspirations. Notice that Elisha has his servant set the small amount of food before the one hundred men, they all eat and they have food leftover; in reality, it was the servant that multiplied the food through the faith and anointing on Elisha. Does this sound eerily familiar to what happened with Jesus?

When Jesus feeds the five thousand, Jesus does the exact same thing. Jesus gives the food to the disciples and ultimately, it was the disciples who continued dividing the food and giving it to all the people until everyone was fed and there was plenty left over.

Like us, Jesus grew up in this cursed world - a world dominated by death and limitations - but thankfully Jesus had those who had blazed trails before Him to give glimpses as to what was possible. I would imagine it was these real life stories Jesus was taught that inspired Him to think beyond what was normal.

Eventually, we know Jesus went beyond these as inspiration and developed a fellowship with God in which God was showing Him what was possible in this alternate reality. God was continually showing Jesus what was possible (John 5:20); when Jesus accomplished it, there were always more limits to push.

JESUS WAS TRAINING OTHERS IN HEAVEN'S REALITY

It's also interesting to note that as God was training Jesus, Jesus was in return training the disciples. The miracles Jesus did were not only for Him, but were also for the disciples training. Jesus was endeavoring to show them what was possible when you live by Heaven's reality.

> Luke 9:51-55 NKJV
> 51 Now it came to pass, when the time had come for Him to be received up, that He steadfastly set His face to go to Jerusalem, 52 and sent messengers before His face. And as they went, they entered a village of the Samaritans, to prepare for Him. 53 But they did not receive Him, because His face was set for the journey to Jerusalem. 54 And when His disciples James and John saw this, they said, "Lord, do You want us to command fire to come down from heaven and consume them, just as Elijah did?" 55 But He turned and rebuked them, and said, "You do not know what manner of spirit you are of.

In Luke 9, James and John ask Jesus if He wanted them to command fire out of Heaven and kill the people. I must say, I absolutely love the fact they (1) thought it was possible and (2) thought they had enough authority to make it happen.

Not only is the response of the disciples interesting but Jesus' response stands out to me as well. *Notice Jesus doesn't rebuke the possibility; Jesus rebukes the motivation.* What kind of person would think they could actually command fire to come out of Heaven? Some of us have a hard time just starting a fire with a match! These guys actually thought it was possible because of what they read about from Elijah and also experiencing the power and authority being displayed through Jesus.

Jesus doesn't tell them that commanding fire out of Heaven wasn't possible. Why? Jesus knew that it was!

2 Kings 1:9-14 NKJV
9 Then the king sent to him a captain of fifty with his fifty men. So he went up to him; and there he was, sitting on the top of a hill. And he spoke to him: "Man of God, the king has said, 'Come down!'" 10 So Elijah answered and said to the captain of fifty, "If I am a man of God, then let fire come down from heaven and consume you and your fifty men." And fire came down from heaven and consumed him and his fifty. 11 Then he sent to him another captain of fifty with his fifty men. And he answered and said to him: "Man of God, thus has the king said, 'Come down quickly!'" 12 So Elijah answered and said to them, "If I am a man of God, let fire come down from heaven and consume you and your fifty men." And the fire of God came down from heaven and consumed him and his fifty. 13 Again, he sent a third captain of fifty with his fifty men. And the third captain of fifty went up, and came and fell on his knees before Elijah, and pleaded with him, and said to him: "Man of God, please let my life and the life of these fifty servants of yours be precious in your sight. 14 Look, fire has come down from heaven

and burned up the first two captains of fifties with their fifties. But let my life now be precious in your sight."

Jesus had read this story as well. Jesus was very aware of what Elijah and Elisha had accomplished. These guys would have been to Jesus what a Smith Wigglesworth and John G. Lake would be to us - inspiration to show what was possible and catalyst to go past what they showed to be possible.

Jesus didn't lecture the disciples and give them a religious talk about why they couldn't do it nor why it wasn't possible. Jesus did not put limitations on His disciples like most of the preachers would do today. Jesus basically said, "Look guys, yes, you could command fire to come out of Heaven, but that is not why we are here."

WHAT MANNER OF SPIRIT ARE YOU

Friend, we must understand what manner of spirit we are. We are born of God; we are sent from Heaven with Heaven's ability to nullify the effect of the curse in the lives of people on the Earth. We have sold ourselves short on what is possible on the Earth. *If James and John thought it was possible to command fire from Heaven, why wouldn't we think it is possible to command a tumor to burn up?*

The difference was that, even in a very short time with Jesus, their mind was being renewed to the possibilities within this alternate reality. They didn't look at the miracles of Elijah as something to be celebrated; they looked at the miracles as something to be replicated.

8

SUBJECT TO CHANGE

The things we see with our natural eye are subject to change; unfortunately, too many of us are being dominated with what we know by our senses instead of what we know by our spirit. Sadly, when it comes to looking at these two realities, we tend to falsely look at the world's reality as absolute.

> 2 Corinthians 5:18 MSG
> There's far more here than meets the eye. The things we see now are here today, gone tomorrow. But the things we can't see now will last forever.

If you can experience it with your senses, it is subject to change. I don't care what it is: it is subject to change. Do you know why? Because the seen things were made from the unseen things. Even physical laws on the earth, although we would consider them absolutes - they are not.

Throughout the Bible, we can read of multiple examples in which physical laws were altered. One such true story was that of Elisha and the widow.

> 2 Kings 4:1-7 NKJV
> 1 A certain woman of the wives of the sons of the prophets cried out to Elisha, saying, "Your servant my husband is dead, and you know that your servant feared the Lord. And the creditor is coming to take my two sons to be his slaves." 2 So Elisha said to her, "What shall I do for you? Tell me, what do you have in the house?" And she said, "Your maidservant has nothing in the house but a jar of oil." 3 Then he said, "Go, borrow vessels from everywhere, from all your neighbors—empty vessels; do not gather just a few. 4 And when you have come in, you shall shut the door behind you and your sons; then pour it into all those vessels, and set aside the full ones." 5 So she went from him and shut the door behind her and her sons, who brought the vessels to her; and she poured it out. 6 Now it came to pass, when the vessels were full, that she said to her son, "Bring me another vessel."And he said to her, "There is not another vessel." So the oil ceased. 7 Then she came and told the man of God. And he said, "Go, sell the oil and pay your debt; and you and your sons live on the rest."

Based on natural law, that is physically impossible; oil doesn't multiply! How was she able to take a small amount of oil and use it to completely fill up multiple jars? By faith, she tapped into Heaven's reality!

DRIVING ON EMPTY

When my son Jake was first born, Lacy and I were living in Bryan, Texas. At that time, I was working for the state of Texas and conducting home inspections for foster parents while also pastoring our church. One day I had to drive over to the city of Bastrop, which was almost 90 miles from our home, to do an 9 pm interview and inspection. Rarely did I do inspections that late, but due to the couple's work hours, this was the only time we could all get together. After I finished the inspection and got back into my car, I noticed the fuel light was on; so, I headed to a gas station that was on my route home just on the edge of town.

When I arrived at the gas station, I pulled out my wallet to get my debit card, but it wasn't there. I then realized I had used it earlier that day and had left it at my house. I began to go through my wallet and found a credit card, but then noticed it had expired. Well, I tried using it anyway, but because of the expiration, it wouldn't process it. I began to rummage through the car to see if I could find any cash, but there was none to be found; however, I found a Walmart gas card. I was relieved at that point because I knew there was a Walmart a few miles away, but it was in the opposite direction I needed to go. The car was running on fumes at this point, but I didn't have a choice; so I headed down the highway to Walmart, praying I would make it there. As I was pulling off the exit ramp to turn into Walmart, my relief of arriving turned into bitter disappointment - this Walmart didn't have a gas station!

I didn't know what else to do, so I drove back to the first gas station. I went inside and told the attendant the situation. I offered to exchange the Walmart gas card to him for cash and he wasn't interested. I then asked if I was to leave my license, if he would allow me to get gas so I could get home and then I would drive back the next day with the money...of which he said, "No."

At this point, I didn't know what to do. I walked back out to the car, sat down and began to talk to God. I said, "God, it is almost midnight. My house is an hour and a half away, I have no money and this Ford Mustang is empty. I didn't do this on purpose and I have tried all I know to do." Suddenly, I was reminded of a story I heard Kenneth Hagin tell about driving on empty. The short version was that he had finished preaching some meetings and didn't have enough money for gas to get home (and he was many hours away from home.) He told his son they would just trust God to get them home. So they got into the car, which was already empty, and drove all through the night on E all the way home.

I thought about it and then said, "God, if you could do that for Bro. Hagin, you can do that for me." So, I rolled down the windows, pulled onto the highway and headed toward Bryan, TX - praying in tongues hard and fast!

Now remember, before I started driving around town trying to get gas, the fuel gauge on the car was already showing empty; there was nothing left in that gas tank as I embarked on my 90 mile faith journey. After driving about thirty minutes down the highway, I knew it was already impossible I had driven that long with no gas, but I kept shoving away the thoughts of myself stranded on the highway in the early hours of the morning. When I hit the thirty minute mark, I started praying in tongues even harder!

After an hour of driving with no gas, my faith was beginning to soar. I knew I only had about thirty minutes to go. When I passed the Bryan city limits sign, I'm not going to lie...I began to shout! I got so excited. I was yelling and stomping my foot on the ground; I was experiencing a manifestation of God's miracle working power. About ten minutes later, I pulled into my driveway a little after 2am just flat out amazed at what God had done for me.

The next morning, I got ready for work and went out to the car; to my amazement, it started up! I drove to a gas station about a mile away and filled it up with 15 gallons of gas. But God! How was it possible that I drove over 90 miles with no gas? I don't know if an angel was pushing it or multiplying the fumes; all I know is God supernaturally took what was impossible in the sense realm and made it possible!

PHYSICAL LAWS CAN BE ALTERED WHEN NECESSARY

The laws of physics are extremely dependable, but even Jesus showed that when needed, these laws could be altered.

A great example is that of Jesus walking on the water. First of all, who told Jesus He could walk on the water? No one that we are told of in the Old Testament did that, so Jesus obviously got this one from the Father; however, isn't it interesting that this miracle inspired Peter that it was possible for him too? Jesus did not tell Peter walking on the water was impossible for him; Jesus invited Peter to experience this alternate reality because it is what man was created to do: dominate the Earth.

Just as with James and John wanting to call fire out of Heaven, Jesus deals with Peter in the same way. Jesus doesn't say, "Peter, you realize that is not impossible?" No, Jesus knew it was possible - it is why He was doing it Himself.

Jesus also was purposefully and intentionally endeavoring to help the disciples access this realm and walk in it too. Jesus never put limits on people as to what was possible in this alternate reality; in fact, Jesus was trying to help them change their perspective and take the limits off!

Just as the prophets of old were inspiration for Jesus, Jesus was doing the same thing for the disciples and raising the standard for what was possible for you and me.

When it comes to the area of healing, you must know that all sickness, disease and physical issues in the body are subject to change. Over time, I have seen so many miraculous healings take place, it has certainly helped renew my mind. You must be able to look at physical things and know, "It is subject to change!"

THE GOITER THAT DISSOLVED IN OKLAHOMA

I'll never forget a time when I was preaching for my friends Pastors Rennie and Pattie Ohl in Warner, OK. During one of the services, we were seeing God do some tremendous miracles, but there was one that has always stood out to me: the woman with the baseball sized goiter on her neck.

I put my hand on the goiter and we cursed it. I pulled my hand back and suddenly, that goiter began to shrink. It was so obvious, Pattie yelled out, "Oh my God! It's shrinking!" Now how does a baseball size growth on someone's body suddenly shrink away to nothing? In the world's reality, it is impossible, but because it is physical, it is always subject to change.

Jesus never looked at a natural situation and saw a situation with no options; Jesus knew it was always subject to change because what was seen was made from what was unseen.

Hebrews 11:2 NLT
By faith we understand that the entire universe was formed at God's command, that what we now see did not come from anything that can be seen.

Why was that tumor subject to change? Because the physical world was made with words, this is where we find the absolute boldness and resoluteness of Jesus. Jesus was extremely aware that where He was from usurped where He was at; if

> *The physical world was made with words; therefore, words can change what is seen.*

what He saw with His physical eyes needed to change, He had the authority to change it.

Obviously, we see the many times Jesus performed miracles of healing, but the miracles that have really been grabbing my attention lately are the miracles with nature and inanimate objects. We know what Jesus did with water: He changed it to wine, calmed it and walked on it. We also know on two occasions, He took a few pieces of bread and fish, multiplied it and fed thousands of people. We also see Jesus curse a fig tree and cause it to die; Jesus then told the disciples that if they commanded the mountain to move, it would obey them.

The one miracle that is never talked about is the stone turning to bread. The reason it is not talked about is because physically it never happened, but *in the mind of Jesus, it already had.* It wasn't just a possibility -it was possible in Heaven's reality and therefore readily available in Jesus' mind.

> Matthew 4:1-4 NLT
> 1 Then Jesus was led by the Spirit into the wilderness to be tempted there by the devil. 2 For forty days and forty nights he fasted and became very hungry. 3 During that time the devil came and said to him, "If you are the Son of God, tell these stones to become loaves of bread." 4 But Jesus told him, "No! The Scriptures say, 'People do not live by bread alone, but by every word that comes from the mouth of God.'"

The reality that turning stone into bread was a very real temptation to Jesus proves that it was possible and doable. Since we know it was possible, imagine the temptation this would have been to Jesus during those forty days. In the wilderness with all of those rocks, there was a bakery waiting to happen! But Jesus stayed the course and used those forty days to dominate His flesh, increase His sensitivity to spiritual things and elevate His fellowship with the Father.

The fact that this potential miracle amazes me proves to me that I still have some renewing of my mind to do in the area of the impossible and this alternate reality! When we begin to see according to this perspective, it totally eliminates fear of lack, fear of death, fear of sickness...fear of anything related to the curse on this earth. Why? Because if it needs to be changed, it can be changed. Why is this possible?

Genesis 1:26-28 NKJV
26 Then God said, "Let Us make man in Our image, according to Our likeness; let them have dominion over the fish of the sea, over the birds of the air, and over the cattle, over all the earth and over every creeping thing that creeps on the earth." 27 So God created man in His own image; in the image of God He created him; male and female He created them. 28 Then God blessed them, and God said to them, "Be fruitful and multiply; fill the earth and subdue it; have dominion over the fish of the sea, over the birds of the air, and over every living thing that moves on the earth."

God gave man dominion not just over the animals but over all of the earth. God's original commission was not only to procreate but also to create and then dominate. Adam was to not only fill it with people but also go out and make the rest of the world look like the Garden of Eden. Jesus not only saw this in the Scripture, but God showed it to Him during those forty days in the wilderness. Jesus wasn't just sitting around on dirt for forty days with hunger pains; Jesus was denying His flesh and also getting direction from God.

Do you really think Moses forty days were better than Jesus forty days? If God showed Moses some things, I guarantee God showed Jesus some things. It is the reason Jesus left the wilderness in power, locked and loaded to manifest Heaven's reality on the Earth. Jesus was ready to do what the Father had shown Him. Jesus was ready to show people there was more to life than what they experienced with their five physical senses. Jesus was coming to reveal an alternate reality from which they could experience abundant life.

9

A LIFE OF ABSOLUTES

We just discussed how everything in this world is subject to change; even the natural laws that do not change can still be suspended when the will of God deems necessary. *When things are subject to change, you can have no faith in them.* Something that is subject to change has no basis for absolute confidence; however, if something is absolute, you can bet your life on it.

Cambridge Dictionary defines *absolute* as "true, right, or the same in all situations and not depending on anything else." This definition of *absolute* is a perfect definition of this alternate reality we are learning about. Heaven's reality is always right and always true.

Remember what Jesus said? "I am the way, the truth (reality) and the life." Heaven's reality is the same in all situations because it has God at the center of it and God does not change. He is faithful and has never told a lie. He is the same yesterday, today and forever!

Hebrews 13:8 NLT
Jesus Christ is the same yesterday, today, and forever.

We also know that God is not dependent on anything; He is self sufficient! As a result, Heaven's reality is a reality of absolutes. Whatever is true in this reality can be counted on with one's life - regardless of what you experience with your five senses in the world's reality.

In a world of chaos, everyone is looking for something to depend on. You can't put your confidence in the stock market. You can't put your trust in the government. Unfortunately, you can't always put your trust in people. When it comes to healthcare, billions of people put their confidence in science and medicine, however, it is always changing and not guaranteed to work for every person in every situation. In addition, as much confidence that science tries to portray, there is not an answer for every physical situation.

> *Where there are no absolutes, there is no peace.*

Watch a commercial for a medication and you will find out quickly that it is not dependable. Yes, for the first fifteen seconds, the spokesperson tells you of all of the medicine's benefits, but the majority of the commercial tells all of the possible side effects: blindness, deafness, heart attack, impotence, seizures, etc. After listening to all the possible side effects, would you put your confidence in that drug? I certainly wouldn't!

When there are no absolutes, there is no peace. You can't have peace of mind when it's possible for something to change or not work - this is one major reason for the fear and anxiety in our world.

However, when it comes to the things of God, there is peace because God does not change. You can bet your life on Heaven's reality because it is not subject to change! In the world's reality, cancer is a death sentence; in Heaven's reality, cancer is just another disease for which Jesus already paid the price.

As we stated earlier, when people get a negative doctor's report such as a cancer diagnosis, the immediate reaction is fear because cancer kills so many people. The world's reality is that cancer kills. This reality that is dominated by the curse and filled with death is viewed by billions around the world as unchangeable. They view physical malformations and chronic diseases as permanent and something people just have to learn how to cope with. The sad thing is they have been duped by Satan because he knows everything in this world is subject to change. Satan doesn't want people to know that because then he loses his biggest weapon: fear.

ABSOLUTES MAKE YOU BOLD

Wouldn't it be wonderful to live life free of fear and anxiety regardless of negative situations in the world? Imagine living in a pandemic and not having the least bit of fear. How could that be possible? It is possible because when you view God's Word, His promises and His realities to be absolute, then you can stare death in the face and laugh knowing that life will prevail.

This is why Jesus could stand before a leper that was missing parts of their body and know with absolute confidence those parts could grow back and the person could be free of leprosy. This is why Jesus put His ministry and reputation on the line so many times. It looked like He was risking it all when in reality, He wasn't risking anything; Jesus was simply seeing and walking according to Heaven's reality.

When you live according to Heaven's reality, you are living according to an absolute. This is why you can sow finances into someone's life and yet, to someone of the world, it looks as though you decreased. What they don't see is that according to Heaven's reality, you just sowed seed and increase is coming back to you. Why? Because in Heaven's reality, there is a spiritual law called Sowing and Reaping and it always works when it is acted upon in faith.

> 2 Corinthians 9:6-10 NLT
> 6 Remember this—a farmer who plants only a few seeds will get a small crop. But the one who plants generously will get a generous crop. 7 You must each decide in your heart how much to give. And don't give reluctantly or in response to pressure. "For God loves a person who gives cheerfully." 8 And God will generously provide all you need. Then you will always have everything you need and plenty left over to share with others. 9 As the Scriptures say, "They share freely and give generously to the poor. Their good deeds will be remembered forever." 10 For God is the one who provides seed for the farmer and then bread to eat. In the same way, he will provide and increase your resources and then produce a great harvest of generosity in you.

I can't tell you how many times Lacy and I have given finances or material things to a ministry or individual and received back much more than we gave away. Whether it was in the form of money, material things or opportunities, the law of Sowing and Reaping always works. This is why even in an up and down economy in the world, our peace stays the same because we know we can live from Heaven's economy which does not change.

As the law of Sowing and Reaping is guaranteed, so is the law of Life. The law of Life is an absolute in Heaven's reality that can always be counted on.

> Romans 8:2 NKJV
> For the law of the Spirit of life in Christ Jesus has made me free from the law of sin and death.

> Romans 8:2 PHILLIPS
> For the new spiritual principle of life "in" Christ lifts me out of the old vicious circle of sin and death.

Just as we have physical laws, there are spiritual laws. Even though science will tell us that physical laws do not change... when God steps in, they can change! As much as there is death in the world, there is more life in Heaven and the spiritual laws of Heaven usurp the laws of this world. The law of Life lifts me out of the old vicious circle of sin and death!

> **Christians who are ruled by their senses will still live a cursed life.**

The law of Life when acted upon will raise the dead, cause a severed spinal cord to become whole, restructure someone's genetic code...what modern medicine says is impossible, the life of God can make possible. The law of Life is a law of this alternate reality and it is why Heaven's reality is an absolute you can bet your life on.

This law will not work unless we renew our mind to the absoluteness of it and make the decision to stop being ruled by our physical senses. Sense ruled people, even though they are Christians and redeemed from the curse, will still continue to live a cursed life.

> Romans 8:5-6 NKJV
> 5 For those who live according to the flesh set their minds on the things of the flesh, but those who live according to the Spirit, the things of the Spirit. 6 For to be carnally minded is death, but to be spiritually minded is life and peace.

As long as people are dominated by the suggestion of their senses, they will be dominated by the curse; yet when we allow our perspective to change and walk according to our spiritual senses, this is when the law of life begins to dominate our daily lives. There is no peace in this world's reality because you can not depend on it!

10

OPTIONS ARE OBSTACLES

The biggest problem in this world's reality is that it is full of options - especially in prosperous countries like America. America is the land of opportunity because it is a land of options. Go to some third world countries and you will not find multiple options of the same food product - you will find one. You won't find multiple colleges to choose from - you may find none. In the arena of health care, America is the land of drugs. There are prescription drugs for everything, including to take care of the side effects of the drugs you're taking to get rid of the first problem!

This is one of the major reasons Bible believing Christians have such a hard time believing God for healing: options. There are many options and as a result, God is usually at the bottom of the list. The world's reality is based on what man can do;therefore, when there is a physical issue, they go to the hospital and usually leave with some type of medication. Sometimes it works and sometimes it doesn't.

That is the problem with the world's systems: there are no absolutes.

Most Christians today, because we haven't been taught properly, have continued to rely on the world's healthcare system that isn't

> *Panic faith is desperation rooted in fear and it doesn't work.*

fail proof. After going through this option and that option, this procedure and that procedure, this medical trial and that medical trial...and doing this for years, they finally turn to God. Unfortunately, for many Christians, when they finally turn to God, they are in what I call "panic faith." They call it "faith" but it's desperation rooted in fear - and it doesn't work.

THE NARROW ROAD

The other day, I was meditating on this subject and spending some time praying in the spirit. I heard these words in my spirit: "Options are obstacles to your faith." The more options you have, the more of an obstacle it will be for you to believe God. Why? Because to follow after God, it requires a narrow focus.

> Matthew 7:13-14 MSG
> 13-14 "Don't look for shortcuts to God. The market is flooded with surefire, easygoing formulas for a successful life that can be practiced in your spare time. Don't fall for that stuff, even though crowds of people do. The way to life—to God!—is vigorous and requires total attention.

The road that is widely traveled is usually the road the world is traveling down. It is wide and has lots of options and doesn't require much attention. Have you ever noticed when you are driving, you pay less attention to what is around you when the roads are wide than when they are narrow? The other day I was driving down a highway with construction in which the road had been narrowed and there were concrete barriers on the edges of the lane. The narrow road required me to slow down and intently focus on how I was driving.

When you are on that narrow road, there are no other options and you are looking straight ahead. When you are on the wide road with multiple lanes, you are looking all around you and there are multiple choices as to what you want to do.

The narrow road requires focus. The wide road allows a free roaming mind.

> Matthew 7:13-14 NKJV
> 13 "Enter by the narrow gate; for wide is the gate and broad is the way that leads to destruction, and there are many who go in by it. 14 Because narrow is the gate and difficult is the way which leads to life, and there are few who find it.

If you find yourself going down the road with lots of people on it, it's probably not the road Jesus paved for you. If you find yourself on the crowded road trying to reach your determined destination, you probably won't make it. Notice Jesus said the wide road is filled with people but it leads to destruction; the narrow road leads to life but it is the road less traveled.

Friend, the road less traveled is usually the one that leads to Jesus and His life!

In this world's reality, when it comes to healing, there is a vast highway filled with billions of people. It is the Medicine Highway and yet there are hundreds of millions of people who die on it.

However, there is a narrow single lane road that has never had one fatality. It is the road of Life and it is a road of absolutes.

Jesus said, "I am the way, I am the truth (reality) and I am the life." Jesus is the reality of what is possible. Jesus is the life, the answer to fulfilling what is possible. Yet, in order to access that life and realize the potential of what Jesus has in Heaven's reality, you must go down Heaven's road for Jesus is THE WAY.

We must be absolute in our belief that Jesus is the only way.

Is Jesus truly the Lord of our bodies?

Thank God for His mercy! He works with us as much as He can while we are growing, but friend, there is coming a day when there will be no other choice but to trust His way.

There is coming a time soon when governments will fail, economies will fail and health systems will fail. During this time, the world will be looking for an answer and that is when we as sons and daughters of God must be able to show THE WAY and manifest the kingdom of God in this world. However, that will never happen unless we begin to travel that road today and develop an absolute trust in Jesus.

ABSOLUTE TRUST

You will find that in Jesus' teachings about the kingdom of God, trust is at the center of this kingdom.

Matthew 6:33 NKJV
But seek first the kingdom of God and His righteousness, and all these things shall be added to you.

Mark 10:24 NKJV
And the disciples were astonished at His words. But Jesus answered again and said to them, "Children, how hard it is for those who trust in riches to enter the kingdom of God!

In this alternate reality, the way it is accessed is by absolute trust. Too many spirit-filled, Bible-believing, healing-believing, tongue-talking believers are trying to talk Heaven's way while living the world's way and wondering why they aren't getting Heaven's results. You can't confess healing scriptures while driving down the wide road with the rest of the world; you need to take the next exit and get on the narrow road that leads to life.

Many of us say we trust God, but do we really? We say that Jesus is our Lord, but is he really? *I would dare say Jesus is certainly the Lord of our spirits, but have we made Him the Lord of our bodies?*

To operate in the reality of absolutes, this reality that always works, it requires absolute trust - it requires Jesus to be our Lord. But how can we sing, "You're all I want, You're all I've ever needed" and yet head off to our next doctor appointment? How do we declare "I believe You're my Healer" and then sit down with the doctor to discuss the next round of chemotherapy treatments?

I do not say these things to bring condemnation on anyone, but at some point, we have to get real about this so we can start seeing the results God wants us to see and we know we should see.

THE TORN ACL

When I was twenty five years old, I was attending Bible school. During a basketball game on the campus, I tore my anterior cruciate ligament in my right knee. No lie...it was the most painful moment I have ever experienced. When that ligament snapped, it was like a gun went off in the gym; everyone in the stands heard it!

I was in such pain, I laid there and cried like a baby while people were rushing down around me on the basketball court. My knee immediately swelled up to the size of a grapefruit and I was taken to the emergency room at the hospital.

The doctor told me my ACL was torn and it would require surgery if I wanted to play sports again. I had a few weeks to think about it as they needed the swelling to go down before they could do surgery. During that time, I had several fellow students tell me, "Forget the surgery; just believe God for healing."

At that time in my life, my faith wasn't there; I just had to be honest with myself. I had gone through a very rough year with school and work. I was only getting about 3 hours of sleep at night because of my job and literally just stayed exhausted all the time. On top of that, it was taking all the faith I had just to pay my bills and get through school...I couldn't take on another faith project.

I'll admit, I did feel a little condemned as I began thinking about the fact I was going to a school that was all about faith in God, but I

90

had to just be real as to where I was at spiritually. I didn't have faith for a miracle in my knee, but I did have faith for a smooth surgery and a super speedy recovery - so that is what I put my faith on.

Sure enough, the surgery went smooth and my physical therapy, which was supposed to last six to nine months only took me three months. The physical therapist told me that in all of his years, he had never seen someone progress so quickly from an ACL injury. Every time I went to my therapy session, he was amazed.

Now, was that God's best for me? No What was God's best? His best was to instantly mend that ligament in my knee, but that would have required my participation. I'm thankful in that situation, medicine was there to bail me out.

FEAR AND HIVES

Now to contrast that, I had a situation happen a few years ago in which I allowed myself to get in to fear - major fear. We were needing several hundred thousand dollars for a church construction project and we needed it in less than a month.

After allowing my mind to run crazy with fear and worry, one day I broke out in hives and my throat began to swell up to the point I was having a hard time breathing. I had no idea at the time what hives were; all I knew was that there were red bumps covering my body and I could barely breath. After a few minutes of arguing about it, Lacy convinced me to go to the hospital.

When we pulled up into the parking lot, I told Lacy, "Give me ten minutes. If I can't get this under control, then I'll let you take me

91

inside to the emergency room" to which she agreed.

As I sat there in the passenger seat, I closed my eyes and began to meditate on the life of God within me. I began to see that life within Jesus flowing in my veins and flowing all throughout my body. Within roughly five minutes, all of the red bumps disappeared and the swelling in my throat went away. I then looked at Lacy a little smugly and said, "Take me home!"

I didn't want to go into that hospital for a number of reasons. (1) I wanted to put into practice what I was teaching. (2) I didn't want a shot. (3) I didn't want to pay out all that money for after hours emergency care!

GOD AND MEDICINE

Thank God for medicine, but it's not God's best. I believe divine health is the grace of God, but medicine is the mercy of God. Do I believe God could show a doctor what is wrong with the body and how to fix it? Certainly! The Holy Spirit is the revealer of truth. Do I believe God would lead someone to go to the doctor? Absolutely. Why? Because the Holy Spirit knows where you are at in your faith and if you aren't there and aren't going to get there, the Holy Spirit knows it.

Yet again, is medicine God's best? Certainly not. How do I know this? Because medicine doesn't always work! The same chemotherapy that helps one person can kill the next person. Surgeries don't always work either. People have died on the surgery table! I just read of someone yesterday who went in for a minor surgery and died later because of complications due to the surgery!

That's why I'm still trying to figure out why people praise God and claim He is the Healer because someone went through multiple rounds of chemo and radiation and came out cancer free. I know that goes counter Christian culture, so don't get offended - just take a step back and listen. God didn't create poison for us to put in our bodies and kill off our immune system. Let's get real. What about those who went into remission and then the cancer comes back? How does one claim God healed

Something is wrong when our healthcare response is the same as the world's healthcare response.

the first time with the chemo and then didn't heal the second time with chemo? The whole concept is crazy!

Just the other day, I saw a spirit-filled church post a "testimony" on social media about God being the Healer. I was excited until I read the rest of the article. The article went on to read, "Brother Joe just got out of the hospital. Brother Joe just got a new shiny pacemaker and came out of surgery singing, "Victory in Jesus." Praise God He is the Healer."

Friend, where is God in our healthcare plan?

Matthew 6:33 NKJV
But seek first the kingdom of God and His righteousness, and all these things shall be added to you.

Yes, Jesus was talking about money and material things in Matthew 6, but it still applies to all the other areas of our life. *But again, if our initial thought is the same as the world's in the area of healing, we must check which reality we are living from.*

In the world's reality, God isn't in the health plan. Cancer? We have chemo for that. Depression? We have a purple pill for that. Fever? We have a white pill for that. Can't sleep? We have pills for that. Flu? We have an immunization for that...but it only works half the time and is only good for the prior years strain. Diabetes? We have a shot for that too!

Now again, this may sound harsh, but it isn't to condemn; however, the Church needs to wake up to the deception we are walking in. I recognize we are all at different places in our understanding, revelation and walk in life. The worst thing you can do is to play the game of "fake faith" and die. **If you are not in faith about the situation, by all means, get yourself to the doctor and get whatever help they can give you** - however, at some point, you need to build yourself up. Start out with an issue that's small in your life and get to the place of being all in.

ALL IN

What do I mean by "all in?" Go all in for Jesus being our Healer. Go all in for Jesus being our Shepherd that keeps us from wanting. Go all in for Jesus being our Protector and Deliverer so that no plague or calamity comes near our bodies. One thousand may fall at one side and ten thousand at another, but it doesn't come near us!

> Mark 13:44 NKJV
> Again, the kingdom of heaven is like treasure hidden in a field, which a man found and hid; and for joy over it he goes and sells all that he has and buys that field.

> Mark 13:45-46 NKJV
> Again, the kingdom of heaven is like a merchant seeking

beautiful pearls, 46 who, when he had found one pearl of great price, went and sold all that he had and bought it.

Heaven's reality requires an "all in" type, a "bet your life on it" type of attitude. Why would someone be like that? Because you know that regardless of how bad the situation looks, God is faithful!

The Bible is full of people who went all in, tapped into Heaven's reality and saw Heaven manifest on the Earth. Take the story of David and Goliath. David, as a teenage boy, went all in to go after Goliath. David literally put his life on the line to defeat what seemed to be an impossible enemy. The odds were stacked against him but before the battle, he already saw the victory as absolute.

1 Samuel 17:34-51 NKJV
34 But David said to Saul, "Your servant used to keep his father's sheep, and when a lion or a bear came and took a lamb out of the flock, 35 I went out after it and struck it, and delivered the lamb from its mouth; and when it arose against me, I caught it by its beard, and struck and killed it. 36 Your servant has killed both lion and bear; and this uncircumcised Philistine will be like one of them, seeing he has defied the armies of the living God." 37 Moreover David said, "The Lord, who delivered me from the paw of the lion and from the paw of the bear, He will deliver me from the hand of this Philistine." And Saul said to David, "Go, and the Lord be with you!" 38 So Saul clothed David with his armor, and he put a bronze helmet on his head; he also clothed him with a coat of mail. 39 David fastened his sword to his armor and tried to walk, for he had not tested them. And David said to Saul, "I cannot walk with these, for I have not tested them." So David took them off. 40 Then he took his staff in

his hand; and he chose for himself five smooth stones from the brook, and put them in a shepherd's bag, in a pouch which he had, and his sling was in his hand. And he drew near to the Philistine. 41 So the Philistine came, and began drawing near to David, and the man who bore the shield went before him. 42 And when the Philistine looked about and saw David, he disdained him; for he was only a youth, ruddy and good-looking. 43 So the Philistine said to David, "Am I a dog, that you come to me with sticks?" And the Philistine cursed David by his gods. 44 And the Philistine said to David, "Come to me, and I will give your flesh to the birds of the air and the beasts of the field!" 45 Then David said to the Philistine, "You come to me with a sword, with a spear, and with a javelin. But I come to you in the name of the Lord of hosts, the God of the armies of Israel, whom you have defied. 46 This day the Lord will deliver you into my hand, and I will strike you and take your head from you. And this day I will give the carcasses of the camp of the Philistines to the birds of the air and the wild beasts of the earth, that all the earth may know that there is a God in Israel. 47 Then all this assembly shall know that the Lord does not save with sword and spear; for the battle is the Lord's, and He will give you into our hands." 48 So it was, when the Philistine arose and came and drew near to meet David, that David hurried and ran toward the army to meet the Philistine. 49 Then David put his hand in his bag and took out a stone; and he slung it and struck the Philistine in his forehead, so that the stone sank into his forehead, and he fell on his face to the earth. 50 So David prevailed over the Philistine with a sling and a stone, and struck the Philistine and killed him. But there was no sword in the hand of David. 51 Therefore David ran and stood over the Philistine, took his sword and drew it out of its sheath and killed him, and cut off his head with it.

Saul tried to offer David the armor and equipment the army used to fight their enemies. It's interesting that the same equipment Saul was confident in giving David, he didn't want to use for himself against Goliath; that's exactly what the world does. Sometimes it works and sometimes it doesn't, but that won't stop the world from using it - because that is all they have. Saul was trying to get David to go down that big wide road they all traveled!

Instead, David went the narrow road and followed the leading of the Holy Spirit. David picked up some stones and then declared the outcome of an impossible situation in the natural.

> 1 Samuel 17:45-47 MSG
> 45-47 David answered, "You come at me with sword and spear and battle-ax. I come at you in the name of God-of-the-Angel-Armies, the God of Israel's troops, whom you curse and mock. This very day God is handing you over to me. I'm about to kill you, cut off your head, and serve up your body and the bodies of your Philistine buddies to the crows and coyotes. The whole earth will know that there's an extraordinary God in Israel. And everyone gathered here will learn that God doesn't save by means of sword or spear. The battle belongs to God—he's handing you to us on a platter!"

NO PLAN B

I love and I mean love what David says at the end. "The whole earth will know there is an extraordinary God in Israel and everyone gathered will learn God doesn't save by means of sword or spear." Do you see it? David was proclaiming that the victory you desire and God wants you to have can only come by going His way, not the world's way. David went all in. He didn't have any back up plan. There isn't a plan B when it comes to faith in God!

> *The victory you desire and God wants you to have can only come by going His way.*

Show me people in the Bible who got miracles with a plan B waiting to be pulled out of their pocket. Did Jesus have a backup plan when He stood before Lazarus grave? If it wouldn't have worked, it would have ruined His ministry! Did Jesus have a backup plan when He was walking on the water? Where were His floaties if He got into fear and began to sink? Where was Elijah's backup plan when he stood on Mt. Carmel facing all the false prophets? Friend, to access the best of what God has for you, you have to go all in.

The greatest miracles I have ever seen happened when I went all in on His way - times where I put myself in a position to look like a complete fool if it didn't work.

THE LADY WITH THE SHORT LEG AND CLUB FOOT

I could fill this book with healing testimonies but there is one I'll share with you along these lines. I'll never forget ministering at a church in Peoria, Illinois in June 2016. I was teaching on our union with Christ and I could tell I was getting nowhere with these people.

After fifteen minutes, I just blurted out, "I can tell this is going nowhere. Let me prove to you that what I'm preaching is true. Who has a back issue?" No lie. I said that to them! As soon as I said it, I realized that was the Holy Spirit helping to stir these people up.

This one particular lady in the center section raised her hand and told me she had some lower back issues. I responded and said, "That will work. Come on up here to the front." As I said that, she said, "Oh by the way, I was born with a short leg and a club foot" and everyone heard it. Well, my first thought was, "I didn't ask for a club foot! I only asked for a simple back issue!" The problem for me was I had already said, "Let me prove to you that what I'm preaching is true." There was no backing out!

So I brought the lady up to the front and sat her down on the platform. She took off her shoe and then I saw how short her leg actually was! I backed off some, pointed at her leg and commanded it to grow.

God is my witness, along with about 150 teenagers and adults in that room...this woman's leg started growing out. Some of the teenagers ran up there with their phones and started recording it as they watched in awe. As soon as that leg grew out to the appropriate length, that club foot started unfolding and became normal!

After that miracle, I had those people locked in! That morning service lasted for four hours as miracles were going off like popcorn kernels in the cooker. Multiple sets of dear ears healed, curved spines healed, a paralyzed face healed, joints and backs healed, people set free from walkers and wheelchairs and tumors dissolved! My God! It was one of the most amazing services I have ever been in...but the catalyst was first going all in. It was a much a lesson for me as it was for the people at the church.

All in on the narrow road of absolutes is a crucial key to accessing Heaven's reality and living in victory while you are in this cursed world.

11

THE POWER IS ALWAYS AVAILABLE

In Heaven's reality, healing power is always available; the power is always on and accessible! Unfortunately, in the Church world we have believed this idea that sometimes the power is on and sometimes it is off.

Luke 5:17-19 NKJV
17 Now it happened on a certain day, as He was teaching, that there were Pharisees and teachers of the law sitting by, who had come out of every town of Galilee, Judea, and Jerusalem. And the power of the Lord was present to heal them. 18 Then behold, men brought on a bed a man who was paralyzed, whom they sought to bring in and lay before Him. 19 And when they could not find how they might bring him in, because of the crowd, they went up on the housetop and let him down with his bed through the tiling into the midst before Jesus.

People are always looking for an excuse to live below where God designed us to live. We are always looking for religious sounding excuses to make up for us not getting the results God intended. There are many that have taken one statement in Luke 5 and have built a doctrine around it. Luke 5:17 says, "...and the power of the Lord was present to heal them." Notice the word present is in italics; this means it wasn't in the original text...the translators added it.

> Luke 5:17 YLT
> And it came to pass, on one of the days, that he was teaching, and there were sitting by Pharisees and teachers of the Law, who were come out of every village of Galilee, and Judea, and Jerusalem, and the power of the Lord was -- to heal them.

The original text says, "And the power of the Lord was to heal them." It has always been God's will for people to be healed and in this situation, God wanted everyone in that house to be healed. This statement isn't telling us about what was available; *this statement was telling us God's desire!* But my oh my - how we have seized on a word that a man added and yet the Holy Spirit didn't say. We took that italicized word, ran with it and began to proclaim miracles could only happen when the anointing was there.

Friend, do you know why the power was there? Because Jesus showed up in the house. There was healing power in that house because the healing power was in Jesus!

> John 14:10 NKJV
> Do you not believe that I am in the Father, and the Father in Me? The words that I speak to you I do not speak on My own authority; but the Father who dwells in Me does the works. 11 Believe Me that I am in the Father and

the Father in Me, or else believe Me for the sake of the works themselves.

Why was the power in Jesus? Not because He was Jesus but because God was in Him. You can not separate God and His power. If God is there, His power is there also. Jesus said it was the Father who dwelled in Him who did the works.

Wherever there is a man or woman filled with God - the power is always available. Now you may not sense that power or even be aware that it is there...but the power is always available. It simply takes someone to recognize t and access it by faith.

> *The power was there because God was in Him.*

In this reality God wants us to live from, we must realize the power is always there. Too many times we are relying on our natural senses to tell us what is possible but faith isn't based on a feeling – faith is based on a knowing. When you know, it will flow!

DON'T BE HOOKED ON A FEELING

Sometimes you may feel the anointing and sometimes you may not. There have been many healing services I have conducted in which I didn't feel anything when I ministered to the person and the person was still healed. There have been times I didn't feel anything and yet the person told me they felt a warmth going through their body. However, there have also been many times I was very much aware of that power and felt it all over me and through me.

Friend, don't be concerned about a feeling. Feelings come and go but the power of God is always there! The more confident you become in understanding that, the more you will begin to see it manifest. I have found the more I think about and talk about the anointing, the more I begin to sense it in my hand. I'll begin to talk about it and sense my right hand begin to burn; as I write this, I feel that sensation in my hand - it is the healing power of God ready to be released!

If you know the power is always available, it will keep you from turning to gimmicks. Do you understand what I mean? I have seen so many church services in which the preacher gets up and prays for God to pour out His power - then it turns into a bunch of hype to try and get something to happen. This is where I honestly just get turned off from church. I know most people mean well, but God doesn't need all of your theatrics and honestly, it turns off those who are truly seeking.

It's been my goal to do everything that I do without fleshly additives. The supernatural doesn't need your natural show! My endeavor is not to get the people hyped up; my endeavor is to connect them with God and get them healed. What you do on the outside has nothing to do with what God put on the inside. *The more you are focused with the outwardly things, the less you will experience the inwardly things.*

The reason people do all of this is because they are trying to get God to release what He already released in their spirit - they just don't know it is there.

Thank God for music. I won't lie...I love some good Gospel

music with the choirs, the bass thumping and the Hammond screaming...but, I don't rely on those things. It's great in church and I am all for doing whatever we can do to help people get from the flesh into the spirit, but we must be very careful we don't set this as the formula for results.

You won't have that music available when you are ministering to someone in the supermarket. You won't have that choir singing for you when you minister to someone in the hospital. And do you know what? Jesus didn't have any of those things either. Jesus did have something that most of us don't - awareness of the power readily available within.

Jesus knew what He had and knew that power was not only readily available but also transferable. It's why He was so confident in giving it to the disciples and then telling them to "Go heal the sick!" It is why Jesus was so confident in declaring the word or laying hands on those who came to Him - because He knew He had the life of God to give away. Jesus was a possessor of that life and subsequently, a releaser of that life.

Now I will admit that we can experience that healing power in various degrees. I've seen it and experienced it in which some services, it seemed like that power was flowing at a ten and others it was flowing at a five. We must understand it is not God holding back - it always comes back to us and our awareness and expectation.

A NIGHT OF MIRACLES, SIGNS AND WONDERS

In March 2019, our church hosted a worship night with gospel artist Todd Dulaney. I was sitting in the sound booth that night just enjoying the worship. Todd and his band were almost through with their set when they began singing a song entitled *Miracles, Signs and Wonders.* They began to sing that song and as I sang the words, it was like I grabbed a hot coal with my hand. I had already been sensing I needed to do something (however, this was not a healing service but a worship service).

I was sitting in the sound booth and debating what to do because this was a worship night and everyone had already been there for almost two hours. While I was contemplating what to do, I began to sense there was someone with ear issues that needed to be ministered to and honestly, I began to debate God.

Well, Todd had finished up and they turned it back over to me. I walked up on the stage and I just couldn't get away from what I knew on the inside. So I told the crowd, "Before we go, is there someone here with some ear issues? The Lord is wanting to heal you."

After a few minutes, a man came down to the front. I put my hands on his ears and he was instantly healed. I didn't ask for it but suddenly a line started forming of people needing healing.

Friend, it was one of the most amazing nights I have ever experienced. Everyone and I mean everyone that I laid hands on was healed. A blind woman was healed. A man with a crushed ankle was healed. A woman with a lump on her stomach the size of a football was healed. A woman who could barely walk was healed and ran all over the auditorium. For a solid hour, it was miracle after miracle! Yet, even amongst all of the miracles, there were still some people in that place that never came up, even though it was obvious they had some physical issues. They saw what was happening but never acted on it.

The healing power of God was there the entire time but it wasn't released until I acted on it. The Holy Spirit prompted me and then I acted as the catalyst in getting things going - but people still had to respond. As in the case of Jesus and the paralyzed man, the healing power of God was available to heal everyone but not everyone received it.

This is why it doesn't make sense to believe that because people didn't get healed, the power wasn't there. Then it gets even more interesting when some people receive healing and others don't... you can't say the power wasn't available. So what do the religious people say? They say, "Well, it must have not been God's time." Like I said earlier, religious people are always looking for a cop out; they are always looking for a religious sounding excuse to cover up their lack of results. It's much easier on our ego to blame God than it is to take personal responsibility.

This is why I believe we just need to simply stick with Jesus. If we just look to Him as our standard, life becomes very simple. I never read of one time in Jesus ministry where before He ministered healing to someone, He first stopped to see if the power was there.

Of course the religious people will always excuse that statement by saying, "Well, but that was Jesus." So then look at when Jesus sent out the twelve disciples; notice in Jesus' command to heal the sick, Jesus never gives them instructions about when the power is present and when it is not. Do you know why? Look at what Jesus told them!

> Luke 9:1-2 NKJV
> 1 Then He called His twelve disciples together and gave them power and authority over all demons, and to cure diseases. 2 He sent them to preach the kingdom of God and to heal the sick.

Jesus said, "I give you power and authority over all demons and to cure diseases." Why would you wonder if the power was there if Jesus gave it to you? Do you see the lunacy in this? So many Christians are praying for the power to show up and not even realizing *it is there when they show up.*

WAITING INSTEAD OF ACTING

How many miracles have been missed because we were waiting instead of acting? How many manifestations of the gifts of the Spirit have been missed because we were waiting on a manifestation before we acted? Friend, faith will get you what the gifts will get you! *You don't have to feel supernatural to manifest the supernatural.* Peter wasn't feeling supernatural when was standing on the boat and looking at Jesus walking on the water. If Peter was basing the supernatural on a feeling, he wouldn't have asked permission; Peter would have simply stepped out and started walking to Jesus!

> *Faith will get you what the Gifts will get you.*

Now I'm not saying you step out on fake faith. Too many times there have been Christians playing fake faith, stepped out of the boat on to the water...and drowned. Do you understand what I'm saying? Whether its financial or physical, many Christians have missed it by playing faith games and yet not truly believing with their heart. But when you know that you know...you can step out in faith and the Holy Spirit will always back you up.

Not only did Jesus not have a "make sure the power is there" conversation with the twelve disciples, He didn't have it with the seventy disciples either.

> Luke 10:1-2, 8-9 NKJV
> 1 After these things the Lord appointed seventy others also, and sent them two by two before His face into every city and place where He Himself was about to go. 2 Then He said to them, "The harvest truly is great, but the laborers are few; therefore pray the Lord of the harvest to send out laborers into His harvest. Do not go from house to house. 8 Whatever city you enter, and they receive you, eat such things as are set before you. 9 And heal the sick there, and say to them, 'The kingdom of God has come near to you.'

Jesus sent them out with the command of "Heal the sick!" There was no talk of limitations. Jesus didn't tell them, "Go heal the sick...but, remember, you only have an anointing for blind eyes and deaf ears." Jesus also didn't tell them, "Go heal the sick, but make sure you spend enough time praying for the power to show up." Jesus fully expected results for every sickness and disease they encountered because He gave them power to get the job done. Jesus' command was not to wait on the power; Jesus' command was to go into the city and release the power!

As much success as the disciples had, it was not to compare to the success in the supernatural that you and I were to have. When Jesus sent out the twelve and the seventy, they were still living under the Old Covenant - yet look at the results they got in healing the sick and casting out devils! Even though they had authority and power, it wouldn't compare to what was coming for them. Look at what Jesus said.

> John 14:16-17 NKJV
> 16 And I will pray the Father, and He will give you another Helper, that He may abide with you forever—
> 17 the Spirit of truth, whom the world cannot receive, because it neither sees Him nor knows Him; but you know Him, for He dwells with you and will be in you.

The Holy Spirit has been with you and will be in you! Well, when Jesus arose from the death victorious and took His seat at God's right hand, it was finished! The Holy Spirit came to reside in the new creature in Christ and when the Holy Spirit came in, the power came to reside and stay!

As a Christian, wherever you go, the power is! You have dead raising power on the inside of you!

> Ephesians 1:19-20 AMP
> 19 And [so that you will begin to know] what the immeasurable and unlimited and surpassing greatness of His [active, spiritual] power is in us who believe. These are in accordance with the working of His mighty strength 20 which He produced in Christ when He raised Him from the dead and seated Him at His own right hand in the heavenly places.

It's amazing to me that even in some of our spirit filled, Charismatic circles, we sing songs about this dead raising power within us and then later on, ask God to pour out His healing power for our bodies! I just sit there and shake my head; yet it is no wonder we do not see the miracles we should be seeing in our churches. We don't believe what the Word says and certainly don't believe what we sing either!

Never forget that Jesus is the Vine and you are the branches; what flows in Him flows in you. In this alternate reality, even in the midst of chaos, the power is always there! Wherever you go, the kingdom of God is ready to manifest and be experienced; however, the only way it will be is for you to act on it. *For the power to be seen, you must know it is already there; otherwise, you will be sitting there, twiddling your thumbs and waiting on God.*

Just keep looking at Jesus. Jesus didn't do much of what we do today that we call faith. Jesus knew who He was, what He possessed, what He was sent to do and Who was with Him. I sum it up like this: position, possession, purpose and presence. These are what I call the four "P's" that we teach in The Healing Academy. Jesus didn't send you into this demonic world for you to get into a situation and then wonder if the power is there.

Friend, please know this: the power is always available! Our job is to simply hear from the Holy Spirit as to what to do in the situation and then act on His instructions. When you do that, Heaven will be on display every single time.

12

ALL POWER AND AUTHORITY

When Jesus walked the earth, He performed some pretty astounding miracles. After the Holy Spirit came upon Jesus in the Jordan River and then spent forty days being tempted, Jesus left the wilderness as a powerhouse!

Luke 4:14-15 NKJV
14 Then Jesus returned in the power of the Spirit to Galilee, and news of Him went out through all the surrounding region. 15 And He taught in their synagogues, being glorified by all.

Jesus healed the blind, deaf, paralyzed and raised the dead; there was no sickness, disease or physical malformity Jesus did not heal. Not only did Jesus perform healing miracles, He worked miracles, signs and wonders with nature. Jesus turned water into wine, multiplied food, calmed a storm and walked on water. When Jesus was praying on the mountain, there was such a degree of glory flowing out of Him, His entire body began to shine. When Jesus stood before the hundreds of soldiers in the Garden of Gethsemane and declared, "I Am", there was so much power released that all the soldiers were knocked to the ground and some of the dead in the area were raised back to life! It is safe to say that Jesus certainly walked in a tremendous amount of power!

SENDING OUT THE TWELVE

While Jesus' ministry was growing, Jesus appointed twelve of the disciples to go preach and heal the sick like Jesus was doing.

> Luke 9:1-2 NKJV
> 1 Then He called His twelve disciples together and gave them power and authority over all demons, and to cure diseases. 2 He sent them to preach the kingdom of God and to heal the sick.

Notice Jesus gave them power and authority over all demons and to cure diseases. First of all, you can't give someone something you don't have; the authority and power Jesus was walking in is the power and authority He gave to the twelve to walk in. Jesus gave them what He had. Second, notice this power was enough to subdue ALL demons and ALL diseases. Jesus didn't send them out into the world to heal the sick, but only be able to heal some sicknesses. Can you imagine going to a group of people, telling them about the goodness of God and then saying, "Jesus will heal you...well, only certain types of diseases." That would be very unChristlike!

Well, the twelve disciples obviously received what Jesus gave them and believed it because Luke 9:6 says, "So they departed and went through the towns, preaching the gospel and healing everywhere." The healing power Jesus gave them was getting results just as if it was Jesus!

SENDING OUT THE SEVENTY

As the ministry continued to grow, Jesus appointed seventy more disciples to go preach the kingdom and heal the sick.

Luke 10:1,9 NKJV
1 After these things the Lord appointed seventy others also, and sent them two by two before His face into every city and place where He Himself was about to go.9 And heal the sick there, and say to them, 'The kingdom of God has come near to you.'

After the seventy returned from their ministry trip of preaching the kingdom of God, healing the sick and casting out devils, they returned with a great report!

Luke 10:17 NKJV
Then the seventy returned with joy, saying, "Lord, even the demons are subject to us in Your name."

In Luke 9 and 10, we see two groups of people, both given the power and authority Jesus had. They go out to preach, heal the sick and cast out devils and get the same results as Jesus. These disciples weren't saved, they didn't have the Holy Spirit living on the inside of them...some of them even got offended at Jesus later on and left Him! However, notice what they accomplished with the authority Jesus had over all disease and all demons!

In John 14, we find Jesus in the upper room giving the disciples some powerful teaching about His union with the Father and what would be possible once they received salvation.

> John 14:10-12 NKJV
> 10 Do you not believe that I am in the Father, and the Father in Me? The words that I speak to you I do not speak on My own authority; but the Father who dwells in Me does the works. 11 Believe Me that I am in the Father and the Father in Me, or else believe Me for the sake of the works themselves. 12 "Most assuredly, I say to you, he who believes in Me, the works that I do he will do also; and greater works than these he will do, because I go to My Father.

It astounds me that even though Jesus said, "You will do the same works and greater works that I did," people still want to say that we can't. Almost every time, the excuse is used that Jesus was God on the Earth and had more of the Holy Spirit than us.

JESUS DID LIFE AS A MAN

It's extremely important to remember that Jesus did all of this as a man. Jesus walked on this Earth with a brain and a body like you and I. Jesus didn't have any more special equipment than you and I which allowed Him to perform the miraculous like He did. His union with God qualified Him and the anointing equipped Him.

> Acts 10:38 TPT
> Jesus of Nazareth was anointed by God with the Holy Spirit and with great power. He did wonderful things for others and divinely healed all who were under the tyranny of the devil, for God had anointed him.

Jesus healed the sick, raised the dead, cast out devils, multiplied food, calmed storms and walked on water *as a man unified with God and anointed by God.* Jesus laid aside everything that gave Him an advantage in life, humbled Himself and did life as a man (Philippians 2:5-6).

So many times, people look for ways to find a way out as to doing the works of Jesus. Go to the vast majority of Christian preachers and I guarantee you will hear excuses as to why the works of Jesus can not be done or excuses as to why we aren't getting results. Rarely will those excuses have humanity as the culprit; almost always it will be some spiritual sounding statement about God holding out.

One of those excuses is found in John 3:34.

John 3:34 NKJV
For He whom God has sent speaks the words of God, for God does not give the Spirit by measure.

People have taken this statement from John the Baptist and used it as a great excuse as to why we can't do the works of Jesus...even though Jesus said we can. This single statement has been pulled out of the Bible and used as an excuse contrary to what the rest of the New Testament tells us. Great ministry leaders have said, "See, Jesus had the Holy Spirit without measure, but you and I have the Holy Spirit with a measure. This is why Jesus could do what He did."

Friend, that's a bunch of religion. Humanity is like water: always looking for the path of least resistance. Our human nature will always look for an excuse as to why we can not measure up to the standard of Jesus Christ...and then our preachers will help us out by taking scriptures out of context to validate it. Most of us have been religiously brainwashed and it is one of the top reasons why we are not seeing the miraculous in the Church like the Bible tells us that we should.

You can't do the works of Jesus without the same equipment.

Let's just use some common sense. You can't do the works of Jesus without the same equipment! Plus, all of the men and women under the Old Covenant didn't have the Holy Spirit living in them. The prophet, priest and king were the only ones to have the Holy Spirit upon them in order to do a certain work. Up until the time of Jesus, it wasn't possible for anyone to have all of the Holy Spirit.

Now, I understand Jesus is the Head of the Church. Jesus Christ stood and stands in all five ministry offices (apostle, prophet, pastor, evangelist and teacher). From this position, you could say that He has the anointing of the Holy Spirit without measure; this is without any dispute.

In that position, He will always stand alone, but as representatives of Heaven, we stand together. He is the Vine and we are the branches; however, what flows in Him, flows in us!

Jesus was the first to walk on the earth full of the Holy Spirit... and He wouldn't be the last either!

Jesus goes on to explain this even more in John 14.

John 14:15-20 NKJV

15 "If you love Me, keep My commandments. 16 And I will pray the Father, and He will give you another Helper, that He may abide with you forever— 17 the Spirit of truth, whom the world cannot receive, because it neither sees Him nor knows Him; but you know Him, for He dwells with you and will be in you. 18 I will not leave you orphans; I will come to you. 19 "A little while longer and the world will see Me no more, but you will see Me. Because I live, you will live also. 20 At that day you will know that I am in My Father, and you in Me, and I in you.

Jesus tells the disciples that on the day of salvation, the same union He has with the Father, they will have with the Father and the Holy Spirit that lives in Him will live in them! Jesus had the Holy Spirit without measure and after salvation, all of us could have the Holy Spirit without measure too! The Holy Spirit would not just be upon us but be within us! We would be wall to wall, floor to ceiling, filled and overflowing with the Spirit of God!

DOING THE GREATER WORKS

So up to this point, we have established that Jesus was doing life as a man anointed by God and had authority and power over all sickness, all disease, all demons and over the earth. Jesus then gives this power to the disciples and they went out and replicated the ministry of Jesus with that same power. Jesus then makes an astounding statement in John 14 and says, "Whoever believes in Me will do the same works and even greater works because I'm going to the Father."

Jesus tells us that because of salvation, we will do the same works and even greater works. To simply find people who believe we can do the same works of Jesus is hard enough; to find people who believe we could do greater...it's almost impossible.

Most theologians say that when Jesus referred to greater works, Jesus meant greater works in quantity. Why? Simply due to the fact that since there would be more Christians, we would be able to accomplish more in number - BUT THIS ISN'T WHAT JESUS SAID! Jesus said we would do greater works...case closed. You don't need the Hebrew and Greek on this; Jesus meant what He said.

Now I know you are sitting there reading this and saying, "Chad, are you actually telling me we can do even greater signs, wonders and miracles than Jesus did on the earth?" Why yes I am! Now, don't close the book and throw it away...let me prove this to you through Scripture.

Friend, I'm telling you, we have sold ourselves short on our salvation. God wants us and needs us to get this revelation because people are dying and going to Hell. This last great move of God is dependent on us grabbing hold of who God has made us to be and the equipment Jesus gave us to use.

GREATER GLORY AND AUTHORITY

While Jesus was praying in the upper room, carefully look at what Jesus says.

John 17:1-5 NKJV
1 Jesus spoke these words, lifted up His eyes to heaven,

and said: "Father, the hour has come. Glorify Your Son, that Your Son also may glorify You, 2 as You have given Him authority over all flesh, that He should give eternal life to as many as You have given Him. 3 And this is eternal life, that they may know You, the only true God, and Jesus Christ whom You have sent. 4 I have glorified You on the earth. I have finished the work which You have given Me to do. 5 And now, O Father, glorify Me together with Yourself, with the glory which I had with You before the world was.

Notice Jesus says, "You have given Me authority over all flesh." We have seen throughout the Gospels that Jesus had authority and power but notice what Jesus says in verse 5.

John 17:5 NKJV
And now, O Father, glorify Me together with Yourself, with the glory which I had with You before the world was.

This right here is proof Jesus was not walking in all that was available. *Jesus said the glory He had before He came to the earth was greater than what He had on the earth.* If you want a second proof of this truth, we find it in no other greater place than in the Great Commission.

Matthew 28:18-20 NKJV
18 And Jesus came and spoke to them, saying, "All authority has been given to Me in heaven and on earth. 19 Go therefore and make disciples of all the nations, baptizing them in the name of the Father and of the Son and of the Holy Spirit, 20 teaching them to observe all

things that I have commanded you; and lo, I am with you always, even to the end of the age." Amen.

After Jesus was crucified, went to Hell, defeated Satan and stripped him of his authority, Jesus arose victorious and now stands before the disciples to make a major announcement: "All authority has been given unto Me. Now take it and go use it!"

Before the resurrection, Jesus was operating under the Old Covenant and using some power and authority. Now after the resurrection, Jesus was operating under the New Covenant with all power and authority! It is this Jesus that you and I are connected with! We aren't unified with the last Adam; we are unified with the glorified Christ who has all power and all authority!

> *Jesus wants to work through us to do even greater works on the Earth.*

Now hold onto your seat because this is where it gets really good! Jesus did everything He did in His earthly ministry with a lesser power and authority than He has now. Now let me take it a step further: Jesus did everything He did on the earth with a lesser degree of power and authority than you have right now!

This is why Jesus said we would not only do the same works but even greater works! Why? Because we would have greater power and authority!

Now I am not saying we are better than Jesus; that would be stupid. We are nothing without Him and can do nothing without Him. Jesus is the Vine and we are the branch and without Him, we can produce no fruit. However, because of our unification with Him, as He is, so are we! We are one with the glorified Christ.

Jesus didn't come to put us on the same level as Adam. God walked with Adam but didn't live in Adam. Jesus came to make a brand new breed of being: a Christ-man filled and flooded with God to walk on this earth with absolute dominion over the earth, with all authority and all power - to the same degree Christ has right now. Jesus is the one who said we could do the same works and even greater works!

Most people don't even believe that statement. Of the few that do, they have tried to wrap their brains around it and find scripture to get them out of doing it. For those that do believe what Jesus said, they have only allowed themselves to try to attain to doing the same works. *But friend, under the new covenant, doing the same works Jesus did under the old covenant is a lower form of Christian living!*

Jesus wants you and I to go past what He did! *Jesus wants to work through us and do even greater works on the Earth* than what Jesus did Himself on the earth.

NO EXCUSES

Jesus showed us what was possible with a lesser degree of power and authority so that we would have no excuses. If a lesser degree of power and authority dominated every single sickness, every single disease and every single demon, we would have no excuse on this Earth to not dominate this cursed reality. This my friend is why the Bible tells us that we are more than conquerors!

With God all things are possible and for the believer, all things are possible. We are dependent on God as the source of power but God is dependent on us to believe we have it.

> Ephesians 3:20 NKJV
> Now to Him who is able to do exceedingly abundantly above all that we ask or think, according to the power that works in us

> Ephesians 3:20 TPT
> Never doubt God's mighty power to work in you and accomplish all this. He will achieve infinitely more than your greatest request, your most unbelievable dream, and exceed your wildest imagination! He will outdo them all, for his miraculous power constantly energizes you.

> Ephesians 3:20 AMP
> Now to Him who is able to [carry out His purpose and] do superabundantly more than all that we dare ask or think [infinitely beyond our greatest prayers, hopes, or dreams], according to His power that is at work within us.

We believe God can do great things! The apostle Paul tells us God can do superabundantly above all we could dare ask or think; however, notice this is dependent on the power that is in us! *What kind of power? All power! This wasn't possible before the resurrection - but now it is!*

THINK BIG

Begin to let your imagination run wild! What is possible for the man/woman filled with God, standing on the earth with all authority and power over the earth? Don't let your mind simply settle on the miracles you read about of the earthly conquests of Moses, Joshua, Elijah, Elisha, Jesus or the disciples. Lift your eyes up to Heaven and begin seeing through the eyes of the glorified Christ. Begin to see things from His perspective and begin to see what is possible!

The only limit to the power is your perspective. As long as you think like a cursed man, you will see cursed results. As long as you think like a religious man, you will see religious results. But when you begin to think like a God man, you will begin seeing God results!

In this alternate reality, in the kingdom of God, we rule on the Earth with absolute dominion. No devil, no sickness, no addiction, no depression and no curse can rule over us. We stand as Kingdom representatives, ambassadors of Heaven, sons and daughters of the living God to exert the rule of God and manifest the righteousness of God in an unrighteous world. Heaven's reality becomes reality on the Earth when we step into all power and all authority.

When we begin to do this, we will not only experience, but live in the greatest move of God Earth has ever seen. It will not happen because God gave something new. It will not happen because God gave us something more than those in the book of Acts. It will happen because we realized what we have, stop making excuses and then use what He has given us.

13

HEAL THE SICK

The works of Jesus were three fold: preaching, teaching and healing. Jesus knew He was a possessor of the life of God and He knew His purpose; as a result, Jesus used these three avenues to reveal Heaven's reality.

Matthew 4:23-24 NKJV
23 And Jesus went about all Galilee, teaching in their synagogues, preaching the gospel of the kingdom, and healing all kinds of sickness and all kinds of disease among the people. 24 Then His fame went throughout all Syria; and they brought to Him all sick people who were afflicted with various diseases and torments, and those who were demon-possessed, epileptics, and paralytics; and He healed them.

Matthew 9:35 NKJV
Then Jesus went about all the cities and villages, teaching in their synagogues, preaching the gospel of the kingdom, and healing every sickness and every disease among the people.

Jesus preached and taught in order to reveal this alternate reality, but also to produce encounters with God. When Jesus gave them truth, it gave the people something on which they could release their faith. You see, the Word of God, when acted upon in faith, will produce manifestations. However, for those who had a hard time

> *In Heaven's reality, we are not looking for healing because we already have it.*

connecting, Jesus would lay hands on them, speak to the issue or give them a command of faith. Healing was one third of the ministry of Jesus; based on this, it is easy to see that healing was a big deal to Jesus.

The issue of healing is two fold: (1) God absolutely loves people and does not want to see people sick and hurting (2) healing is a physical proof of a supernatural truth.

WE BRING HEALING

In the world's reality, sickness and disease are normal. Taking medications and going to the doctor is normal for people in this world because that is how we have been taught to take care of physical issues. In the world's reality, people are looking for healing, but not so in Heaven's reality. In Heaven's reality, we are not looking for healing because we already have it; instead, our mission changes. Instead of looking for healing, we bring healing; instead of running from the leper, we run to the leper. A virus doesn't get on us; His life leaves us and gets on the virus.

Jesus understood this and it is time the Church understood it too. Jesus was endeavoring to show people this new reality in which they could live from, this alternative reality He referred to as the kingdom of Heaven. Jesus was preaching and teaching about this reality and then helping people experience it firsthand.

Matthew 10:1-13 PHILLIPS
1-4 Jesus called his twelve disciples to him and gave them authority to expel evil spirits and heal all kinds of disease and infirmity. The names of the twelve apostles were: First, Simon, called Peter, with his brother Andrew; James, and his brother John, sons of Zebedee; Philip and Bartholomew, Thomas, and Matthew the tax-collector, James, the son of Alphaeus, and Thaddaeus, Simon the Patriot, and Judas Iscariot, who later turned traitor.
5-8 These were the twelve whom Jesus sent out, with the instructions: "Don't turn off into any of the heathen roads, and don't go into any Samaritan town. Concentrate on the lost sheep of the house of Israel. As you go proclaim that the kingdom of Heaven has arrived. Heal the sick, raise the dead, cure the lepers, drive out devils—give, as you have received, without any charge whatever.
9-10 "Don't take any gold or silver or even coppers to put in your purse; nor a knapsack for the journey, nor even a change of clothes, or sandals or a staff—the workman is worth his keep!
11-13 "Wherever you go, whether it is into a town or a village, find someone who is respected, and stay with him until you leave. As you enter his house give it your blessing. If the house deserves it, the peace of your blessing will come to it. But if it doesn't, your peace will return to you.

Jesus' commission to the twelve was simple: preach the kingdom of Heaven and heal the sick. The twelve disciples had already seen the power and authority Jesus was walking in; they had experienced mighty demonstrations of healing power in Jesus' ministry. They knew what Jesus gave them would work and so they went out and got the same results.

JESUS' COMMANDS AREN'T FILLED WITH REGULATIONS

I want you to notice a few things in Jesus' instructions to the twelve. First, notice Jesus didn't qualify the types of sicknesses and diseases; at no point do we see Jesus talk about small diseases or big diseases. Second, He didn't take the twelve and then start handing out special anointings - a special anointing to heal blind eyes to Peter, a special anointing to heal cancer to Thomas, or a special anointing to James for leprosy. Third, Jesus didn't talk to them about which gifts of the Spirit needed to be in manifestation for particular illnesses or ailments. Remember, with the exception of diversity of tongues and the interpretation of tongues, all the other gifts of the Spirit had already been available and in operation under the Old Covenant.

The things we see ministers do and talk about today in regards to healing, we just don't see much of it in Jesus ministry. Jesus didn't talk to them about creating an atmosphere for the Holy Spirit to move and He certainly didn't talk to them about portals of glory and open Heavens. Jesus simply showed them what the power and authority would do, gave it to them and then told them to go heal the sick.

Not long after the twelve disciples got started on their ministry trips of preaching the kingdom of Heaven, healing the sick and casting out devils, Jesus appointed seventy more disciples to go out and do the same thing.

Luke 10:1,8-9 PHILLIPS

1 Later on the Lord commissioned seventy other disciples and sent them off in twos as advance-parties into every town and district where he intended to go.

2 "There is a great harvest," he told them, "but only a few are working in it—which means you must pray to the Lord of the harvest that he will send out more reapers.

3-7 "Now go on your way. I am sending you out like lambs among wolves. Don't carry a purse or a pair of shoes, and don't stop to pass the time of day with anyone you meet on the road. When you go into a house, say first of all, 'Peace be to this household!' If there is a lover of peace there, he will accept your words of blessing, and if not, they will come back to you. Stay in the same house and eat and drink whatever they put before you—a workman deserves his wages. But don't move from one house to another.

8-12 Whatever town you go into and the people welcome you, eat the meals they give you and heal the people who are ill there. Tell them, 'The kingdom of God is very near to you now.' But whenever you come into a town and they will not welcome you, you must go into the streets and say, 'We brush off even the dust of your town from our feet as a protest against you. But it is still true that the kingdom of God has arrived! I assure you that it will be better for Sodom in 'that day' than for that town.

I find it extremely interesting that when Jesus sends out the twelve and the seventy, *He spends more time giving them instruction on how to respond to people than instructions on how to heal the sick.* You would think that if healing the sick was such a big task, Jesus would have given them a lot of teaching and instruction on it.

However, just as with the twelve, the seventy had been with Jesus in his meetings and healing services. They had seen firsthand the healing power of God on display and the authority Jesus walked in. The seventy disciples knew just as the twelve disciples that the power and authority Jesus gave them would produce. They didn't need coaching; they just needed a commission.

When the seventy returned from their ministry trip, they came back full of excitement because what Jesus gave them produced results. They came back and exclaimed, "Even the demons are subject to us in your name!"

The two biggest differences I see in the command to the twelve and the seventy is that:

> 1. Jesus specifically told the twelve apostles to not only heal the sick but also cast out demons
> 2. Jesus told the seventy to heal the sick and then tell them they had just encountered the kingdom of God.

The response of the seventy tells me they had great results in healing the sick but they were more elated to see the demons respond to their authority in Jesus Name. Think about that: unsaved men with a commission and faith in their possession - they got people healed of diseases and free of demonic forces.

It's also interesting to me in Jesus' command to the seventy.. the command was simple: heal the sick. Once the people were healed, then the disciples were to tell them, "You just experienced the kingdom of God." In this situation, the disciples were to heal first and then explain - this seems like a far cry to what we see today.

Now I'm certainly not putting down our times of teaching and preaching; again, this was two thirds of Jesus ministry. Teaching and preaching the Word will certainly bring about faith for people to receive and act on the Word which will produce manifestations; however, there are times when people need to see first and then hear.

Remember the story I told you about the women with the club foot? That service was a perfect illustration of this truth. I was teaching those people about some of these realities we are talking about, but they weren't getting it. When I stopped teaching and gave the Holy Spirit an opportunity to demonstrate, the manifestations opened up their heart to receive.

MIRACLES NOW

There will be many times in which you encounter people that need a miracle - NOW! They don't have time for you to try to teach faith into them for several months; they may only have two weeks to live! What if you come upon an accident and someone is at the point of death? What are you going to do - have a Bible study? No! You heal the sick! We must be like the twelve and the seventy and be confident in the mission Jesus gave us to heal the sick.

When I was six years old, my dad was in a terrible car accident. He was driving to work very early in the morning before sunlight. As he was driving down this dark road in a wooded area, suddenly he saw the flash of a man's face. Before my dad could even hit his brakes, his car hit a man in the middle of the road; the man was flipped into the windshield and then bounced off of it and fell onto the side of the road.

My dad pulled off to the side of the road and heard someone yelling for help; it was a friend of the man who was hit. My dad located him a little ways back and said he could hear the one cursing and moaning in pain and the other yelling for help. Once he located them in the dark, he said the first thing that came to mind was to ask the man if he wanted prayer. My dad got down beside him, put his hand on him and prayed for him in the name of Jesus. Not too long after that, an ambulance arrived and took both of the men to the hospital.

Later on that day, I remember sitting at the kitchen table in our house on Pevitot Road in Beaumont, Texas. I remember as a seven year old boy seeing my dad very distraught over what had happened as he told us the story of hitting the man with the car. While we were sitting there, he got a phone call and it was the mother of the man who was hit. The mother explained the two men were drunk and playing their own version of Russian Roulette - trying to dodge cars in the dark.

To my dad's amazement, the mother told him the only thing that was wrong with her son was he had a broken thumb. Friend, that was a miracle! My dad's car was smashed to pieces in the front, the windshield was completely broken and there was blood all over the front of the windshield. The fact the man survived being hit head on by that car is astounding; how he walked away with only a broken thumb...that was power and authority that produced a miracle. What was even better...that young man ended up receiving Jesus as his Savior!

Can you imagine what would have happened had my dad reacted

like most people? Most people would have stood before the man and would have hoped for God to do something; instead, my dad didn't react - he responded with his God given authority and spoke life into that man's body.

THE DUAL WORKING OF GOD AND MAN

You will never find Jesus ask God to heal the sick. Nowhere will you find Jesus teach the disciples to ask God to heal the sick. Why? Because God gave the authority to man. This is a truth we see not only in the new covenant, but also under the old covenant.

Exodus 14:13-21 NKJV
13 And Moses said to the people, "Do not be afraid. Stand still, and see the salvation of the Lord, which He will accomplish for you today. For the Egyptians whom you see today, you shall see again no more forever. 14 The Lord will fight for you, and you shall hold your peace." 15 And the Lord said to Moses, "Why do you cry to Me? Tell the children of Israel to go forward. 16 But lift up your rod, and stretch out your hand over the sea and divide it. And the children of Israel shall go on dry ground through the midst of the sea. 17 And I indeed will harden the hearts of the Egyptians, and they shall follow them. So I will gain honor over Pharaoh and over all his army, his chariots, and his horsemen. 18 Then the Egyptians shall know that I am the Lord, when I have gained honor for Myself over Pharaoh, his chariots, and his horsemen." 19 And the Angel of God, who went before the camp of Israel, moved and went behind them; and the pillar of cloud went from before them and stood behind them. 20 So it came between the camp of the Egyptians and the camp of Israel. Thus it was a cloud and darkness to the one, and it gave light by night to the

other, so that the one did not come near the other all that night. 21 Then Moses stretched out his hand over the sea; and the Lord caused the sea to go back by a strong east wind all that night, and made the sea into dry land, and the waters were divided.

Moses gave a strong statement of faith as to what God was going to do, but God wasn't pleased. Instead, God rebuked Moses! Why? Because God had given Moses the anointing and He expected Moses to do something with it.

God responded to Moses and said, "Why are you complaining to Me? Take your rod and you divide the sea!" Now, did Moses divide the Red Sea all by himself? No, we see that when Moses stepped out on his authority and released the anointing, God caused the sea to divide. This was a dual working of God and man.

Just as God told Moses, "You divide the sea," Jesus told us, "You heal the sick!" In the same way, we are not the healer; God is the Healer. However, for God to move on the Earth, He moves through us.

> John 5:17 NKJV
> But Jesus answered them, "My Father has been working until now, and I have been working."

> John 14:10,11 NKJV
> 10 Do you not believe that I am in the Father, and the Father in Me? The words that I speak to you I do not speak on My own authority; but the Father who dwells in Me does the works. 11 Believe Me that I am in the Father and the Father in Me, or else believe Me for the sake of the works themselves.

This was the case with Jesus on the Earth; Jesus and the Father were working together. You never see Jesus ask God to do it; Jesus moved in faith and in His moving, the Holy Spirit moved and backed Him up.

This is where we must be cautious in our thinking and never lose sight of our position and yet out utter dependency on Jesus. In one sense, we are the healer because we are the deliverers on the Earth; we are Christ on the Earth. However, we can do nothing without Him. It is a dual working together of us and Jesus. You must see yourself as the deliverer in any situation you encounter in which someone needs a touch of God. You must know that Jesus has sent you to heal the sick and in that commission is the provision to accomplish the mission.

People would say, "Well Chad, I hear what you're saying but that was only for the twelve and the seventy disciples." Believe me - I've heard it for years! However, this wasn't just for the twelve and the seventy; this was for the believer!

John 14:12 TPT
I tell you this timeless truth: The person who follows me in faith, believing in me, will do the same mighty miracles that I do—even greater miracles than these because I go to be with my Father!

I love, love, love this view of John 14:12: "I tell you this timeless truth." This is a timeless truth of this alternate reality: whoever believes in Jesus will do the same mighty miracles He did and even greater miracles because of salvation. The work of every believer is not only to pray, not only to disciple others and not only to financially support the Gospel, but also to heal the sick.

Friend, this is for every believer! Now I know there are those that Jesus, as the Head of the Church, has appointed to the ministry of healing. There is no denying that. The apostle Paul tells us in 2 Corinthians that of those called to the fivefold ministry, there are those who have been anointed in that area - but don't let that excuse you out of a life of fun!

Yes, there are those especially anointed by Jesus to lead in the ministry of healing, but every believer has been called to lay hands on the sick and bring healing. Jesus didn't qualify the believers in John 14:12. Jesus didn't say it was for the mature saints or those called to a ministry office. Jesus said every believer would do the same works and greater works...and some of those works include healing! Why?

ALL HAVE BEEN CALLED

For those who want to intellectually try to debate themselves out of John 14:12, there is no way they excuse themselves from what we know as the Great Commission.

Mark 16:15-20 TPT
15 And he said to them, "As you go into all the world, preach openly the wonderful news of the gospel to the entire human race! 16 Whoever believes the good news and is baptized will be saved, and whoever does not believe the good news will be condemned. 17 And these miracle signs will accompany those who believe: They will drive out demons in the power of my name. They will speak in tongues. 18 They will be supernaturally protected

from snakes and from drinking anything poisonous. And they will lay hands on the sick and heal them."19 After saying these things, Jesus was lifted up into heaven and sat down at the place of honor at the right hand of God! 20 And the apostles went out announcing the good news everywhere, as the Lord himself consistently worked with them, validating the message they preached with miracle-signs that accompanied them!

Who is supposed to go into all the world and preach the Gospel? All of us! We have all been called to the ministry! It doesn't matter if you are Baptist, Catholic, Presbyterian, Lutheran, Church of God... we are all called to go into our world and preach the good news of the kingdom of God. Just as with the twelve and the seventy, not only are we to tell people about the kingdom, but we are also to cast out devils and heal the sick.

In all three of Jesus commands to heal the sick, Jesus simply gives the command. Why? Because the power and authority of Heaven's reality over this world's reality is so great, it doesn't require any effort on your part. We are simply the vessel allowing the Miracle worker to flow through us.

We are the ones who have made healing extremely difficult. We have bought into the reality of this world that healing is hard. The Church has bought into the world's reality that healing and miracles are abnormal. *Instead of looking through Jesus' eyes, we have looked through the world's eyes and then tried to find Scriptures to back it up. This is why we have struggled in the area of healing.*

All throughout the Gospels, there is only one time we see the disciples not get the same results of Jesus; in that instance, it was not due to an ability issue but a connection issue.

> Matthew 17:14-21 NKJV
> 14 And when they had come to the multitude, a man came to Him, kneeling down to Him and saying, 15 "Lord, have mercy on my son, for he is an epileptic and suffers severely; for he often falls into the fire and often into the water. 16 So I brought him to Your disciples, but they could not cure him." 17 Then Jesus answered and said, "O faithless and perverse generation, how long shall I be with you? How long shall I bear with you? Bring him here to Me." 18 And Jesus rebuked the demon, and it came out of him; and the child was cured from that very hour. 19 Then the disciples came to Jesus privately and said, "Why could we not cast it out?" 20 So Jesus said to them, "Because of your unbelief; for assuredly, I say to you, if you have faith as a mustard seed, you will say to this mountain, 'Move from here to there,' and it will move; and nothing will be impossible for you. 21 However, this kind does not go out except by prayer and fasting."

DOMINION WITHOUT ABSOLUTES DO NOT WORK

Do you see it? Look at Jesus response through non religious eyes. Jesus didn't tell them they weren't anointed enough to heal the young boy. Jesus didn't tell them they didn't have the right gifts in operation. Jesus explanation was simple: Unbelief. Now I know church folk don't like that word because it puts responsibility on our shoulders; most Christians would rather blame God or the devil instead of look at themselves in the mirror.

You can not exert dominion without absolutes. This is why this issue of being all in and removing the options is so important in Heaven's reality. There are no shades of gray, no either/or; it's yes or no. It must be known that it will be done for the healing power to flow and be received.

When it came to lack of results, Jesus didn't remind them about their humanity. This wasn't an equipment failure; this was a connection failure! Jesus talked to them about unbelief and then went onto to talk about the need of prayer and fasting. This issue of prayer and fasting is the connection issue - staying connected and aware of the Holy Spirit revealing and speaking to us what to do in a given situation.

Friend, see things from Jesus' perspective!

Colossians 3:1-3 NLT
1 Since you have been raised to new life with Christ, set your sights on the realities of heaven, where Christ sits in the place of honor at God's right hand. 2 Think about the things of heaven, not the things of earth. 3 For you died to this life, and your real life is hidden with Christ in God.

When we heal the sick, we are seeing from Heaven's perspective and then allowing Heaven to invade Earth. We died to the world's way of healing and now have a new way of healing according to Heaven's reality.

Heaven's reality is full of health. There is no sickness in Heaven and God doesn't want sickness on the Earth. The first Adam brought sickness into the Earth by his sin. The last Adam defeated sickness in the Earth by His righteousness. The Christ men and women are to enforce Jesus' victory by telling the world of Heaven's reality and then manifest it by setting people free by healing those that are sick spiritually, mentally and physically.

HEALING THE SICK IS NOT HARD

Jesus command of "Heal the sick" reveals not only His heart but also the reality of Heaven that healing is not some monumental task. If it was hard, Jesus would have told us so. If it would have required years of spiritual maturity, Jesus wouldn't have chosen the people that He did. "Heal the sick" was not reserved for those with degrees in theology or flamboyant personalities; it is a command given to all of those who are living in this alternate reality. Healing the sick is a command of compassion for the cursed world that is sick and dying. It is part of the commission for those sent from Heaven to allow the will of Heaven to be done on the Earth.

14

GRAVES AND DEATH BEDS

In the last chapter, we spent some time talking about Jesus' commands to the disciples. Remember, these were not just commands for the twelve or the seventy; these commands were for all disciples of Jesus, including you and me.

Matthew 10:7-8 NKJV
7 And as you go, preach, saying, 'The kingdom of heaven is at hand.' 8 Heal the sick, cleanse the lepers, raise the dead, cast out demons. Freely you have received, freely give.

There is one piece of Jesus' command that I want to take some time on and that is the command of raising the dead.

Death is one of those things in this natural life that when it occurs, it is an absolute. Once someone is dead, they are dead and there are no more options - but again, we are talking about death in regards to the world's reality. In Heaven's reality, death wasn't even supposed to be an issue on the Earth. Death was not in the original creation package; however, due to the curse, things changed and death became a natural part of life.

Now, even though death is part of this natural life, we must understand that with everything else in this natural realm, God still has authority over it and because God had authority over it, Jesus had authority over it.

> John 5:21 NKJV
> For as the Father raises the dead and gives life to them,
> even so the Son gives life to whom He will.

Jesus said He could give life to whoever He willed. That's a powerful statement and one that is absolutely absolute. Jesus lived a life of absolutes and saw everything as black and white; there is no gray area with Jesus. He saw every disease as curable and He saw everyone in the grave as raisable. Think about it for a moment. The power that flowed in Jesus could have lifted every single dead body out of the graves in Israel with just a word.

We have on record Jesus raising three people from the dead:

- The widow of Nain's son (Luke 7:11-17)

- Jairus' daughter (Luke 8:49-56)

- Lazarus (John 11:1-44)

There is also the young boy who was raised from the dead in the Garden of Gethsemane. It isn't talked about much but it is recorded in Mark 15:51-52. Simply by the power that flowed out of Jesus when He declared "I AM," it not only knocked the soldiers on their backs but also raised at least one from the dead.

Outside of the three on record that Jesus raised from the dead, there are many others for which we have Scriptural accounts.

Elijah: the widow of Zarephath's son

1 Kings 17:17-23 NKJV
17 Now it happened after these things that the son of the woman who owned the house became sick. And his sickness was so serious that there was no breath left in him. 18 So she said to Elijah, "What have I to do with you, O man of God? Have you come to me to bring my sin to remembrance, and to kill my son?" 19 And he said to her, "Give me your son." So he took him out of her arms and carried him to the upper room where he was staying, and laid him on his own bed. 20 Then he cried out to the Lord and said, "O Lord my God, have You also brought tragedy on the widow with whom I lodge, by killing her son?" 21 And he stretched himself out on the child three times, and cried out to the Lord and said, "O Lord my God, I pray, let this child's soul come back to him." 22 Then the Lord heard the voice of Elijah; and the soul of the child came back to him, and he revived.23 And Elijah took the child and brought him down from the upper room into the house, and gave him to his mother. And Elijah said, "See, your son lives!"

Elisha: the Shunammite woman's son

2 Kings 4:32-35 NKJV
32 When Elisha came into the house, there was the child, lying dead on his bed. 33 He went in therefore, shut the

door behind the two of them, and prayed to the Lord. 34 And he went up and lay on the child, and put his mouth on his mouth, his eyes on his eyes, and his hands on his hands; and he stretched himself out on the child, and the flesh of the child became warm. 35 He returned and walked back and forth in the house, and again went up and stretched himself out on him; then the child sneezed seven times, and the child opened his eyes.

Dead man thrown on Elisha's bones

2 Kings 13:20-21 NKJV
20 Then Elisha died, and they buried him. And the raiding bands from Moab invaded the land in the spring of the year. 21 So it was, as they were burying a man, that suddenly they spied a band of raiders; and they put the man in the tomb of Elisha; and when the man was let down and touched the bones of Elisha, he revived and stood on his feet.

Saints in Jerusalem raised at Jesus death

Matthew 27:50-53 NKJV
50 And Jesus cried out again with a loud voice, and yielded up His spirit.51 Then, behold, the veil of the temple was torn in two from top to bottom; and the earth quaked, and the rocks were split, 52 and the graves were opened; and many bodies of the saints who had fallen asleep were raised; 53 and coming out of the graves after His resurrection, they went into the holy city and appeared to many.

Jesus raised from the dead

Matthew 28:1-8 NKJV
1 Now after the Sabbath, as the first day of the week began to dawn, Mary Magdalene and the other Mary came to see the tomb. 2 And behold, there was a great earthquake; for an angel of the Lord descended from heaven, and came and rolled back the stone from the door, and sat on it. 3 His countenance was like lightning, and his clothing as white as snow. 4 And the guards shook for fear of him, and became like dead men. 5 But the angel answered and said to the women, "Do not be afraid, for I know that you seek Jesus who was crucified. 6 He is not here; for He is risen, as He said. Come, see the place where the Lord lay. 7 And go quickly and tell His disciples that He is risen from the dead, and indeed He is going before you into Galilee; there you will see Him. Behold, I have told you." 8 So they went out quickly from the tomb with fear and great joy, and ran to bring His disciples word.

Peter: Tabitha raised from the dead

Acts 9:36-41 NKJV
36 At Joppa there was a certain disciple named Tabitha, which is translated Dorcas. This woman was full of good works and charitable deeds which she did. 37 But it happened in those days that she became sick and died. When they had washed her, they laid her in an upper room. 38 And since Lydda was near Joppa, and the disciples had heard that Peter was there, they sent two men to him, imploring him not to delay in coming to them. 39 Then Peter arose and went with them. When he had come, they brought him to the upper room. And all the widows stood by him weeping, showing the tunics and garments which Dorcas had made while she was

with them. 40 But Peter put them all out, and knelt down and prayed. And turning to the body he said, "Tabitha, arise." And she opened her eyes, and when she saw Peter she sat up. 41 Then he gave her his hand and lifted her up; and when he had called the saints and widows, he presented her alive.

Paul: the raising of Eutychus

Acts 20:7-12 NKJV
7 Now on the first day of the week, when the disciples came together to break bread, Paul, ready to depart the next day, spoke to them and continued his message until midnight. 8 There were many lamps in the upper room where they were gathered together. 9 And in a window sat a certain young man named Eutychus, who was sinking into a deep sleep. He was overcome by sleep; and as Paul continued speaking, he fell down from the third story and was taken up dead. 10 But Paul went down, fell on him, and embracing him said, "Do not trouble yourselves, for his life is in him." 11 Now when he had come up, had broken bread and eaten, and talked a long while, even till daybreak, he departed. 12 And they brought the young man in alive, and they were not a little comforted.

The fact that all of these people were raised from the dead is proof that death is not always an absolute. It proves that death was not part of the divine plan of God for the Earth. It also shows what is possible by a man or woman filled and united with God.

Notice that some of the accounts took place by people who weren't even saved under the old covenant! We see another instance of a dead man being thrown on the bones of Elisha and that man being raised from the dead.

This is one of the reasons Jesus was confident that death didn't have to be an absolute in every situation. You could say that Jesus was absolute in his belief that death did not have to be an absolute! Jesus had seen in the Old Testament Scripture that this was possible. Through His meditation of those scriptures, along with His encounters with God, it built in Him an absolute, unshakeable confidence that death just wasn't that big of a deal.

> Luke 7:11-15 NKJV
> 11 Now it happened, the day after, that He went into a city called Nain; and many of His disciples went with Him, and a large crowd. 12 And when He came near the gate of the city, behold, a dead man was being carried out, the only son of his mother; and she was a widow. And a large crowd from the city was with her. 13 When the Lord saw her, He had compassion on her and said to her, "Do not weep." 14 Then He came and touched the open coffin, and those who carried him stood still. And He said, "Young man, I say to you, arise." 15 So he who was dead sat up and began to speak. And He presented him to his mother.

THE RESPONSE OF JESUS

You can tell a lot about what people truly believe by the way they respond to a situation. It doesn't seem that Jesus knew about this funeral; He just happened to come upon it. The compassion of Jesus towards this widow moved Him to move.

Jesus didn't put on a big show nor give a long prayer. Jesus didn't need special music nor need everyone to get quiet and create an atmosphere of miracles. Jesus didn't check to see if certain gifts of the Spirit were in operation or if there was an open Heaven. Jesus knew His position, His possession, His purpose and the fact that God's presence was with Him. By a simple command of authority, Jesus spoke seven words: "Young man, I say to you arise."

Isn't it interesting Jesus spoke to the dead man as if the man was alive? You will find that Jesus never responded to the situation as it was; Jesus responded as it should be. Jesus wasn't responding to this funeral according to the sense realm; Jesus responded according to the Heaven's realm.

You can tell when someone is responding to the sense realm in a religious manner; they quote scriptures and say spiritual things all while responding emotionally to the situation.

Friend, there is always peace and joy when responding according to the spirit. *In Heaven's reality, we are always in control of the situation - even with death;* as a result, our emotional response is not the same as the sinner for our emotional response is in response to our spirit.

> Mark 5:35-43 NKJV
> 35 While He was still speaking, some came from the ruler of the synagogue's house who said, "Your daughter is dead. Why trouble the Teacher any further?" 36 As soon as Jesus heard the word that was spoken, He said to the ruler of the synagogue, "Do not be afraid; only believe." 37 And He permitted no one to follow Him except Peter, James, and John the brother of James. 38 Then He came to the house of the ruler of the synagogue, and saw a

tumult and those who wept and wailed loudly. 39 When He came in, He said to them, "Why make this commotion and weep? The child is not dead, but sleeping." 40 And they ridiculed Him. But when He had put them all outside, He took the father and the mother of the child, and those who were with Him, and entered where the child was lying. 41 Then He took the child by the hand, and said to her, "Talitha, cumi," which is translated, "Little girl, I say to you, arise." 42 Immediately the girl arose and walked, for she was twelve years of age. And they were overcome with great amazement. 43 But He commanded them strictly that no one should know it, and said that something should be given her to eat.

When Jesus was approached about Jairus' daughter, Jesus said with confidence He would go and heal her. Upon hearing the girl is now dead, notice Jesus' response does not change. Jesus

> *In Heaven's reality, we are always in control of the situation - even with death.*

doesn't say, "I was going to heal her sickness, but now that she is dead, well, there is nothing we can do." No, Jesus continues on. *Why would the fact that the girl died change the mission?* Do you see this my friend?

Jesus' perspective did not change simply because the situation changed in this world's realm. However, you can see in this example how Heaven's perspective and the world's perspective are on opposite spectrums.

Mark 5:35-36 NKJV
35 While He was still speaking, some came from the ruler of the synagogue's house who said, "Your daughter is dead. Why trouble the Teacher any further?" 36 As soon as Jesus heard the word that was spoken, He said to the ruler of the synagogue, "Do not be afraid; only believe."

When Jairus' servants saw the girl had died, that was the end of the story for them. Notice they were fine waiting for Jesus to come heal the daughter but as soon as she died, from their perspective, there was no sense in bothering Jesus anymore. However, Jesus response to Jairus is powerful. As soon as Jesus heard the death report that was spoken, Jesus looked at Jairus and said, "Do not be afraid; only believe." In other words, Jesus was telling Jairus to not change his belief. *If Jairus wasn't allowing the sense realm to move him out of faith when the girl was sick, why should he allow the sense realm to move him out of faith now that the girl was dead?*

Sometimes while I am reading, I use my imagination to see these stories. If I was watching it as a movie in my mind, I can see it right now. Immediately after hearing the girl had died, Jesus spins Jairus towards Him, gets face to face with him and with absolute calmness, boldness and assuredness, (and a cinematic orchestra playing in the background) looks at Jairus and says, "It isn't over!" and then begins to walk with a swagger in slow motion towards Jairus house. Well, at least that's the way I would write it!

STAY IN THE FAITH REALM

What we have in this story is Jesus endeavoring to hold Jairus in the realm of faith by those powerful words of assurance. If you can keep yourself in the faith realm, you will win every situation, but if you allow yourself to get into the sense realm, you will lose every situation. No one has ever won a faith fight while focused on the world's reality.

This is why Jesus responded to Jairus' daughter the way He did. Jesus knew He already won the situation before He even arrived at the house. When Jesus does arrive, He says, "Why are you all weeping? The girl is only

> *No one has ever won a faith fight while focused on the world's reality.*

asleep." For this statement, Jesus is ridiculed but what else would you expect from people living according to this world's reality? Yet this shows us something else about the perspective of Jesus when it came to death. *Jesus saw raising someone from the dead just as easy as waking someone up from a nap.*

WHAT YOU SEE AS BIG WILL REQUIRE BIG

I firmly believe this is why we have not seen people raised up from the dead in situations in which they should. Some people have been bold to go raise people up from a death bed but went into it seeing it as something big. That's the key difference. Jesus saw death as little; we see it as big.

When you see a situation in this world as big, then it's going to take big faith and big prayers (and if we are like most people, sending out requests on social media for as many people as we can to pray because we don't believe our connection to God is strong enough.)

Think about it for a moment. When you face a situation in life that seems small to you, how many times do you ask people to pray about it with you? Contrast that to when you face something that seems big to you - how many times do you ask people to pray about it with you?

I'm certainly not putting down the power of prayer nor the prayer of agreement, but what I am trying to deal with is our perspective. Most of the time, we are looking for people to pray, not out of confidence based on the Scripture, but out of fear, based on the situation.

We must get back to Jesus' perspective, especially in this area. Jesus had absolute control and confidence in this area and we should as well. Why? *Because raising the dead was part of Jesus' commission to us as His disciples.*

> Matthew 10:5-8 MSG
> 5-8 Jesus sent his twelve harvest hands out with this charge: "Don't begin by traveling to some far-off place to convert unbelievers. And don't try to be dramatic by tackling some public enemy. Go to the lost, confused people right here in the neighborhood. Tell them that the kingdom is here. Bring health to the sick. Raise the dead. Touch the untouchables. Kick out the demons. You have been treated generously, so live generously.

Jesus not only gave the command to heal the sick but also raise the dead. Up until this point, they had been with Jesus for a while and had seen marvelous miracles firsthand. Peter, James and John in particular were with Jesus in the room when He raised Jairus' daughter from the dead. They saw the calmness and authority that He walked in through every adverse situation, now including death. Jesus had given the twelve disciples authority to heal the sick, raise the dead and cure the incurable.

IN THE COMMISSION IS THE PROVISION

In Jesus' commission was the provision to get the job done. Jesus wouldn't have sent them out to do what He did if He didn't believe they had what it took. The authority and power Jesus was walking in, He gave to the disciples to replicate His works.

Notice again Jesus didn't talk about particular gifts of the Spirit that were needed. Jesus doesn't talk about creating an atmosphere of miracles. Jesus understood that when the Holy Spirit is with you, all the gifts that are needed are always available because the Holy Spirit is there. Jesus understood that when you are filled with God, the atmosphere changes with your arrival. Jesus understood that when a righteous man shows up, all unrighteousness must bow. Jesus understood that the life of God in Him was greater than the death on the outside of Him. Jesus understood that light always conquers darkness.

> *Jesus understood that when you are filled with God, the atmosphere changes with your arrival.*

Matthew 11:28-30 MSG
28-30 "Are you tired? Worn out? Burned out on religion? Come to me. Get away with me and you'll recover your

life. I'll show you how to take a real rest. Walk with me and work with me—watch how I do it. Learn the unforced rhythms of grace. I won't lay anything heavy or ill-fitting on you. Keep company with me and you'll learn to live freely and lightly."

THE COMMANDS OF JESUS AREN'T HEAVY

Anything Jesus sends us to do, it is from the place of authority and in the repeated patterns of grace. I love the Message translation of this passage in which Jesus says, "I won't lay anything heavy or ill fitting on you...live freely and lightly." Why should the command to heal the sick and raise the dead put a weight on us? The only reason it could possibly become a weight is when we step out of grace and step into works.

Condemnation is simply the result of you not seeing yourself as good enough. If we are honest, in and of ourselves, we are not good enough to work miracles; however, we are not alone. When we received salvation and became united with Christ, we ceased being two and became one. We are one spirit with the Lord (1 Corinthians 6:17). Therefore, we are absolutely perfect and complete in Him (Colossians 2:9-10).

We are the righteousness of God in Christ and we have Him working miracles through us. *If the situation puts a weight on you, it's because you stopped seeing yourself in Christ and you put the weight on yourself.*

If raising the dead seems to be a big deal to you, it is not because it is a big deal; *it is because you made it to be a big deal.* You are allowing death to seem bigger than a cold. You are allowing death to seem bigger than a headache. You are allowing death to seem bigger than Christ in you.

There is a powerful story John G. Lake tells about raising a baby from the dead; yet, the story isn't about him raising the baby up; it is about his unbelief.

> One day I sat in Los Angeles, talking to old father Seymore. I told him of an incident in the life of Elisa Letwaba, one of our native preachers in South Africa. I went to his home and his wife told me that he had gone to pray for a little baby who had been hurt. So we went over and I got down on my knees and crawled into the native hut. I saw he was kneeling in a corner. I said, "Letwaba, it is me. What is the matter with the child?" He told me that the mother had the child in a blanket, as natives carry their children and it fell out and he thought it had hurt its neck. I examined it and saw its neck was broken. I said to Letwaba, "Why, Letwaba, the baby's neck is broken." It would turn from side to side like the neck of a doll.

> I did not have the faith for a broken neck, but poor old Letwaba did not know the difference. He discerned the spirit of doubt in my soul. I said to myself, "I am not going to interfere with his faith. He will just feel the doubt generated by all the old traditional things I ever learned, so I will go out." I went and sat in another hut and kept on praying. I lay down at 1a.m. At three, Letwaba came in.

> I said, "Well, Letwaba, how about the baby?" He looked at me so lovingly and sweetly and said, "Why, brother,

the baby is all well." I said, "The baby is well! Letwaba, take me to the baby at once." So we went to the baby and I talked to the little black thing on my arm and I came out praying, "Lord, take every cursed thing out of my soul that keeps me from believing in the Lord Jesus Christ." And Mr. Seymour shouted, "Praise God, brother, that is not healing, it is life." (Adventures with God. page 253)

Lake's response to the situation was according to the world's reality. Upon seeing the child's broken neck, Lake immediately was pulled from the faith realm, of which he naturally resided as a Christian, into the sense realm of which he was redeemed from and was to rule over. I appreciate Lake's honesty and transparency with this because it shows us that even a man who had seen such tremendous miracles as he had, even Lake at times allowed himself to get into unbelief and not experience the God encounters he should have experienced.

When we look at the story of Lazarus being raised from the dead, we see these same types of responses from those involved.

John 11:5-15 NKJV
5 Now Jesus loved Martha and her sister and Lazarus. 6 So, when He heard that he was sick, He stayed two more days in the place where He was. 7 Then after this He said to the disciples, "Let us go to Judea again." 8 The disciples said to Him, "Rabbi, lately the Jews sought to stone You, and are You going there again?" 9 Jesus answered, "Are there not twelve hours in the day? If anyone walks in the day, he does not stumble, because he sees the light of this world. 10 But if one walks in the night, he stumbles, because the light is not in him." 11 These things He said, and after that He said to them, "Our friend Lazarus

sleeps, but I go that I may wake him up."12 Then His disciples said, "Lord, if he sleeps he will get well." 13 However, Jesus spoke of his death, but they thought that He was speaking about taking rest in sleep.14 Then Jesus said to them plainly, "Lazarus is dead. 15 And I am glad for your sakes that I was not there, that you may believe. Nevertheless let us go to him."

First of all, notice again Jesus compares Lazarus death to that of sleep. In verse 11, Jesus is speaking from Heaven's perspective and says, "Our friend Lazarus sleeps, but I go that I may wake him up." We can see why Jesus was so calm and matter of fact about these types of situations; He simply saw it differently because He was living from Heaven while living on the Earth.

Don't ever forget John 3:13 in which Jesus said, "No one has ascended to heaven but He who came down from heaven, that is, the Son of Man who is in heaven." Jesus was living from this alternate reality on the Earth - the one you and I are to be living from as well.

Jesus speaks from His perspective but the disciples don't understand; they were still dealing with a cursed mindset, being sense ruled and being accustomed to this world's reality. They responded by saying, "If he is asleep, then he will wake up and be fine." So Jesus has to get down on their level and speak according to their worldly understanding. Jesus says, "Look guys, I'm keeping my mindset where it needs to be, but you aren't helping. Lazarus isn't asleep; he is dead, but I'm going to raise him up."

It's important who is in the company you keep; in most situations, we wouldn't want to be around people that aren't believing, but in this situation for Jesus, it was training for the guys who would take the ministry of Jesus around the world.

When Jesus gets to Bethany, He encounters Martha, who in many ways typifies the modern Christian.

> John 11:20-27 NKJV
> 20 Then Martha, as soon as she heard that Jesus was coming, went and met Him, but Mary was sitting in the house. 21 Now Martha said to Jesus, "Lord, if You had been here, my brother would not have died. 22 But even now I know that whatever You ask of God, God will give You." 23 Jesus said to her, "Your brother will rise again." 24 Martha said to Him, "I know that he will rise again in the resurrection at the last day."25 Jesus said to her, "I am the resurrection and the life. He who believes in Me, though he may die, he shall live. 26 And whoever lives and believes in Me shall never die. Do you believe this?" 27 She said to Him, "Yes, Lord, I believe that You are the Christ, the Son of God, who is to come into the world."

Martha's first words to Jesus were, "If you would have been here, Lazarus wouldn't have died." We can see where Martha's faith was at; her faith was in Lazarus being healed, not in Lazarus being raised from the dead.

Jesus endeavors to redirect her from the sense realm back to the faith realm by saying, "Martha, your brother will rise again." Instead of Martha passing the test, she fails miserably. She immediately pivots from what isn't possible in her mind to what is possible in her mind: Lazarus being raised upon Jesus' second coming. Jesus again tries to move her into faith by saying, "I am the resurrection and the life!" Remember what Jesus said in John 5?

John 5:21,26-27 NKJV
21 For as the Father raises the dead and gives life to them, even so the Son gives life to whom He will. 26 For as the Father has life in Himself, so He has granted the Son to have life in Himself, 27 and has given Him authority to execute judgment also, because He is the Son of Man.

Jesus was letting her know that even in the midst of death, life was available because He was there.

When Martha leaves, she goes to Mary. Mary, who was usually the more spiritual of the two, unfortunately responds the exact same way.

John 11:28-35 NKJV
28 And when she had said these things, she went her way and secretly called Mary her sister, saying, "The Teacher has come and is calling for you." 29 As soon as she heard that, she arose quickly and came to Him. 30 Now Jesus had not yet come into the town, but was in the place where Martha met Him. 31 Then the Jews who were with her in the house, and comforting her, when they saw that Mary rose up quickly and went out, followed her, saying, "She is going to the tomb to weep there." 32 Then, when Mary came where Jesus was, and saw Him, she fell down at His feet, saying to Him, "Lord, if You had been here, my brother would not have died." 33 Therefore, when Jesus saw her weeping, and the Jews who came with her weeping, He groaned in the spirit and was troubled. 34 And He said, "Where have you laid him?" They said to Him, "Lord, come and see." 35 Jesus wept.

Upon Mary's grief and those who followed her, we see Jesus moved with compassion. Friend, Jesus wasn't crying because He was sad; He already knew He was going to raise Lazarus up! The compassion of the Lord is a powerful thing and something I have experienced several times. Friend, I'm not much of an emotional person, but when the love of God moves on you and through you for someone else, I've wept like a baby in front of a whole bunch of people.

Jesus stood before the grave and commands the stone to be rolled away. We see Mary silent, but once again, Martha speaks up and continues to reveal her life perspective which is ruled by a cursed mindset of impossibilities.

> John 11:38-40 NKJV
> 38 Then Jesus, again groaning in Himself, came to the tomb. It was a cave, and a stone lay against it. 39 Jesus said, "Take away the stone." Martha, the sister of him who was dead, said to Him, "Lord, by this time there is a stench, for he has been dead four days." 40 Jesus said to her, "Did I not say to you that if you would believe you would see the glory of God?"

I think it is safe to say that no one in this entire situation was in faith except for Jesus. Martha's response for why Lazarus couldn't be raised was, "He's so dead that His body stinks!" Since when did a bad smell stop the power and life of God from flowing?

His Heavenly perspective allowed Jesus to release life into what seemed an absolutely impossible situation. Lazarus wasn't just dead a few hours like Jairus' daughter or a day like the widow's son; Lazarus had been dead for four days. However, Jesus fully believed that even after four days of death, it was possible. It would also be the miracle that would ultimately lead to the death of Jesus but it also proved to Jesus that Him being raised up in three days was not only possible, but doable.

Before we close this chapter, I want to say that I do understand there are some factors in people being raised from the dead. We must be led by the Holy Spirit. In no way am I advocating haphazardly going into funeral services and trying to raise people up from the dead when you have no leading of the Lord.

We can in many ways do more harm than good in these situations if we miss it. There were many people who died during the three years of Jesus ministry and obviously, Jesus didn't go and raise all of them up from the dead. We can see this in the area of healing itself. You can look at the story of the man healed at the pool of Bethesda; Jesus, being led by the Holy Spirit, intentionally went to that one man. We never see Jesus healing every single person at the pool; Jesus was led to this particular man.

We also must realize that the will of that person is involved as well. Unless the Lord reveals it to you, the reason the person died is between that person and the Lord, but if we are honest with ourselves, no one who has been in Heaven face to face with Jesus would want to come back to the Earth. I can tell you from personal experience that when the Lord took me to Heaven in October 2005, I didn't want to come back!

A great example of this situation was told by Smith Wigglesworth about his wife Polly, in which she died and Smith raised her up.

"Good-bye Polly," said Wigglesworth as he sent her off to preach. 'Smith, watch me when I'm preaching. I get so near to heaven when I'm preaching that some day I'll be off.' He thought back on these words that his dear Polly had once spoken. 'Well,' he mused, 'she certainly must have preached tonight.'

It was New Year's Day, 1913, and the local doctor and a policeman had met him just as he was stepping out the front door on his way to Glasgow to minister at some meetings. However, the look on the two men's faces as they met him told him that something was wrong. 'Polly's dead, Smith. She fell dead at the mission door.' Just a few hours before he had bid her well as she was leaving to go preach there.

How he loved his Polly. She was everything in the world to him. In the natural he was devastated , but deep down inside, he knew that she was where she wanted to be. He began to speak in tongues and praise the Lord, laughing in the Spirit.

Soon the house was filled with people. Her body had been brought to the house. At Smith's instructions, they took her up to her room and laid her lifeless form on the bed. 'She's dead, and we can do no more.' Smith just smiled. He knew differently. Asking everyone to please leave the room, he closed the door when the last one had left. He turned around and walked over to her bed . He knew that she was with her beloved Lord as she had so longed to be, but standing before her now he couldn't bear the separation. 'In the name of Jesus, death give her up.' Polly's eyes opened and looked straight into his. 'Polly, I need you.' She answered, 'Smith, the Lord wants me.'

An incredible struggle was going on inside him now. Oh, how much he wanted her with him. How could he go on without her? He had thought that they would have so many more years together. That still small voice came- the voice he knew so well, the only one he loved more than hers. 'She's mine. Her work is done.' With tears streaming down his face , he yielded to his Lord. 'My darling, if the Lord wants you, I will not hold you.' She smiled as he kissed her cheek tenderly. Then he simply said, 'Good-bye for the present.' Her eyes closed, and she was gone . 'Yes Lord.' He had obeyed. He turned and walked out of the room. It was the hardest thing he had ever done. (The Wigglesworth Standard. pg 143-144. Whitaker House)

Smith Wigglesworth had a legal right in this situation with his wife. Jesus had a legal right in the situation with Jairus because Jairus gave Him authority to do so with that child. I am of the firm belief that when someone with spiritual authority in a situation comes to us in faith, it legally opens the door for us to move on their behalf.

There are also many situations in which someone has died young that God was waiting on a bold man or woman in Christ to raise that person up and yet God couldn't find anyone. They didn't finish their race and God still needed them in the race, but He needed an ambassador of Heaven to speak for Him and raise that person from the dead.

We must realize Jesus defeated not only spiritual death but also physical death; physical death is the one piece of the redemption puzzle that has been paid for but has not been delivered and can't be delivered until the end. As a result, this means that we all have to die a physical death unless we are alive when Jesus returns for His Church. Even though we must die a physical death, it doesn't mean we have to die young or sick. We have a choice in the matter and there are situations in which the Lord still needs that person to get a job done; therefore, He needs us to move on His behalf.

We must increase our sensitivity and we must change our perspective of death to that of Jesus Christ Himself. The raising of the dead is part of the ministry of Jesus Christ. It is part of our ministry today as ambassadors of Heaven. Friend, I promise you we will see more of this in our day - not because of God pouring out something extra special, but because a new breed of people, like you and me, are rising up to think and see like Jesus. We have dead raising power already on the inside of us. The same power that raised Jesus from the dead is always at your disposal.

Be led by the Holy Spirit and when He moves on you to raise someone from the dead, remember it's no different than waking them up from a nap. *In this alternative reality, raising people from the dead is normal.*

15

DEATH BY CHOICE

In the world's reality, there is another idea that has been accepted as truth and yet is a lie that's been propagated by Satan for thousands of years. The sinner believed it and the Church bought into it: it is the idea that you have no choice over when you die.

As in most cases, much of the lies pushed by Satan have a little touch of scripture on them. Remember, he is the deceiver. Satan doesn't come out and ask you to drink the poison; he is going to put it on a nice juicy steak!

Job 14:1-5 NKJV
1"Man who is born of woman
Is of few days and full of trouble.
2 He comes forth like a flower and fades away;
He flees like a shadow and does not continue.
3 And do You open Your eyes on such a one,
And bring me to judgment with Yourself?
4 Who can bring a clean thing out of an unclean?
No one!
5 Since his days are determined,
The number of his months is with You;

You have appointed his limits, so that he cannot pass.

Job states in his prayer to God that "his days of life have already been determined by God." This statement came from Job during his nine month affliction by Satan. If you read the entire book of Job, you quickly discover that Job didn't really know what he was talking about. In Job's prayer, he goes on to say that he would be better off for God to kill him and put him in a grave.

> *If God was in control of our lives, everyone would already be saved.*

If this was the only basis for people believing they have no choice in their time of death, then I get it. If it doesn't seem like you have any authority on the earth, then it would seem logical that you have no control over when you take your last breath. Plus, preachers have grabbed hold of this passage of scripture and used it for centuries to put people in the grave - and I'm not just talking about those that have died. Millions of Christians over the years have been "encouraged" by ignorant ministers on their death bed by letting them know "God is in control."

Friend, if God was in control, everyone would be saved and we would all be out of here. Remember in the very beginning, God gave man dominion over the Earth. We are the ones in control, but in far too many cases, we have given that authority over to Satan to use against us.

So does God have our days numbered on a calendar in Heaven? Certainly, God is all knowing and He knows the day we will die, but is that day set because God chose it or because God knows when we will choose it?

Remember, I'm always looking to Jesus. Jesus stated He was reality. Whatever was available to Him is available to me too because of my union with Him. Check out what Jesus has to say about His control over His life.

> John 10:18 NKJV
> No one takes it from Me, but I lay it down of Myself. I have power to lay it down, and I have power to take it again. This command I have received from My Father."

I HAVE THE POWER TO LAY IT DOWN

What a powerful statement! Don't forget, this was Jesus saying this as a man filled with God - which means, we can say the very same thing because we are in the very same position!

Jesus said, "No one can take my life from Me." Now we see this throughout Jesus' earthly ministry. Remember the times in which people tried to kill Him?

> Luke 4:20-21, 28-30 NLT
> 20 He rolled up the scroll, handed it back to the attendant, and sat down. All eyes in the synagogue looked at him intently. 21 Then he began to speak to them. "The Scripture you've just heard has been fulfilled this very day!"28 When they heard this, the people in the synagogue were furious. 29 Jumping up, they mobbed him and forced him to the edge of the hill on which the town was built. They intended to push him over the cliff, 30 but he passed right through the crowd and went on his way.

This church mob started pushing Jesus toward a cliff to kill Him, yet somehow, Jesus passed through the crowd. How is it possible that a group of people detains one person and somehow that person just walks away without any struggle and the people knowing it? It doesn't even say that Jesus ran away - Jesus just casually went His way. Jesus was ALWAYS IN CONTROL.

> John 10:34-39 NKJV
> 34 Jesus answered them, "Is it not written in your law, 'I said, "You are gods" '? 35 If He called them gods, to whom the word of God came (and the Scripture cannot be broken), 36 do you say of Him whom the Father sanctified and sent into the world, 'You are blaspheming,' because I said, 'I am the Son of God'? 37 If I do not do the works of My Father, do not believe Me; 38 but if I do, though you do not believe Me, believe the works, that you may know and believe that the Father is in Me, and I in Him." 39 Therefore they sought again to seize Him, but He escaped out of their hand.

Here again, you have more church people get so mad at Jesus, they try to capture Him to have Him killed, but somehow Jesus slipped through all of their grasp. Why? They couldn't touch Jesus because He was in control of His life.

Let's look again at what Jesus said about His control over His life.

> John 10:18-20 NKJV
> 18 I surrender my own life, and no one has the power to take my life from me. I have the authority to lay it down and the power to take it back again. This is the destiny my Father has set before me." 19 This teaching set off

another heated controversy among the Jewish leaders. 20 Many of them said, "This man is a demon-possessed lunatic! Why would anyone listen to a word he says?"

This is about as plain as it gets. "No one has the power to take my life from me. I have the authority to lay it down and the power to take it back again."

Who had complete authority over Jesus life? Jesus did. Who gave Jesus authority over His life? God did.

Did you notice the response of the people? It set off a firestorm among the people. They thought Jesus had lost His mind! Others claimed He was demon possessed. Sadly, things haven't changed in the last two thousands years. If you were to get up in a church today and proclaim "I have complete authority over my life and I choose when I will die," you would probably get thrown out of the church! They would say, "Who do you think you are?"

Friend, Jesus is the one who said this and God is the one who gave Jesus the authority. This is why no one could touch Jesus the entire time He was on the earth. The only reason He was able to be captured by the over six hundred soldiers in the garden of Gethsemane is because Jesus allowed it!

John 18:3-12 NKJV
3 Then Judas, having received a detachment of troops, and officers from the chief priests and Pharisees, came there with lanterns, torches, and weapons. 4 Jesus therefore, knowing all things that would come upon Him, went forward and said to them, "Whom are you

seeking?" 5 They answered Him, "Jesus of Nazareth." Jesus said to them, "I am He." And Judas, who betrayed Him, also stood with them. 6 Now when He said to them, "I am He," they drew back and fell to the ground. 7 Then He asked them again, "Whom are you seeking?" And they said, "Jesus of Nazareth." 8 Jesus answered, "I have told you that I am He. Therefore, if you seek Me, let these go their way," 9 that the saying might be fulfilled which He spoke, "Of those whom You gave Me I have lost none." 10 Then Simon Peter, having a sword, drew it and struck the high priest's servant, and cut off his right ear. The servant's name was Malchus. 11 So Jesus said to Peter, "Put your sword into the sheath. Shall I not drink the cup which My Father has given Me?" 12 Then the detachment of troops and the captain and the officers of the Jews arrested Jesus and bound Him.

Jesus could have easily escaped this situation if He wanted to escape. If you look at the layout of Jerusalem, Jesus would have seen the lamps and torches of the soldiers as they left the city walls and headed toward the garden of Gethsemane. Jesus willingly stayed to be arrested.

As Jesus stood before the soldiers, when they asked if He was Jesus, Jesus responded by saying, "I Am" and the power of Heaven was released and knocked all of the soldiers on their backs. Even in that moment, Jesus could have ran away if He wanted - but He stayed. Do you really think these guys could have put their hands on Jesus unless He allowed them to?

Finally, Jesus states to Peter, "Shall I not drink the cup which My Father has given Me?" In other words, "Peter, I need to finish what

God has called Me to do." Jesus willingly laid down His authority and allowed Himself to be arrested and crucified."

IT IS FINISHED

John 19:28-30 NKJV
28 After this, Jesus, knowing that all things were now accomplished, that the Scripture might be fulfilled, said, "I thirst!" 29 Now a vessel full of sour wine was sitting there; and they filled a sponge with sour wine, put it on hyssop, and put it to His mouth. 30 So when Jesus had received the sour wine, He said, "It is finished!" And bowing His head, He gave up His spirit.

When Jesus is on the cross, He has literally become the curse for humanity. He is not only suffering from the physical pains of being tortured, beaten and the horrific cruelty of being crucified, He has also taken on the spiritual sin of the world, all the sicknesses of the world and has become spiritually separated from God.

What astounds me about this situation is that, even though being spiritually dead at this point and despite the astounding physical pain Jesus was enduring, He still had control over the situation. Jesus still audacious faith in operation in that, He not only chose to be in the situation, He chose when it would be over.

When Jesus knew that He had completed everything He was sent to do, Jesus declared, "It is finished!" and then intentionally gave up His spirit. Friend, Jesus chose how long to stay on that cross and then chose when to die!

When Jesus said, "No man can take my life; I have the authority to lay it down," Jesus meant it. God Himself gave this command to Jesus.

Now what does this have to do with us? EVERYTHING!

Jesus was the standard for what is available! Yes, we will eventually have to die a physical death but NOWHERE IN THE BIBLE DOES IT SAY I DO NOT HAVE CONTROL!

Jesus never said we have to die from sickness or disease. How could I die from a sickness or disease when Jesus gave me all power and all authority over all sickness and all disease? How could death just decide to take me out when I have dead raising power on the inside of me?

In the world's reality, they don't have much say because they are under the rule of Satan and not under the protection of God; but even as a sinner, they still have authority in their words and they can have what they say.

As the son and daughter of God, we have absolute control over when we die. God promised us one hundred and twenty years my friend!

> Genesis 6:3 NKJV
> And the Lord said, "My Spirit shall not strive with man forever, for he is indeed flesh; yet his days shall be one hundred and twenty years."

SATISFIED WITH LONG LIFE

Not only have we been promised one hundred twenty years. If

you don't want to live to be one hundred twenty years, that is totally up to you. In the world's reality, seventy and eighty years old are the elderly years; not so in Heaven's reality. At eighty years old, that is simply the 2/3 mark for the child of God living from Heaven on the Earth!

Psalm 91:16 NKJV
With long life I will satisfy him, and show him My salvation."

Notice God said He would satisfy us with long life. Is long life thirty years old? Why certainly not. But do you know how many times I have heard preachers say at the funeral of a young adult, "It was God's appointed time for them to die." Either the preacher was wrong or God was totally confused on the definition of long life!

PROLONG YOUR DAYS

Have you ever noticed how many times God gives us instructions on how to increase the length of our life?

Proverbs 3:1-2 NKJV
1 My son, do not forget my law,
But let your heart keep my commands;
2 For length of days and long life
And peace they will add to you.

Deuteronomy 4:40 NKJV
You shall therefore keep His statutes and His commandments which I command you today, that it may go well with you and with your children after you, and that you may prolong your days in the land which the Lord your God is giving you for all time."

Ephesians 6:1-3 NKJV
1 Children, obey your parents in the Lord, for this is right. 2 "Honor your father and mother," which is the first commandment with promise: 3 "that it may be well with you and you may live long on the earth."

If God has an appointed time for us to die, why would He give us instructions on how to lengthen our days? That doesn't make any sense at all! What does make sense is that God gave us choice as to how long we can live within that one hundred and twenty years. The longer we live on the Earth, the more we can do for Him. During our time on the Earth, He wants us to live healthy, wealthy and fully in control. How do we know that? Because Jesus gave Himself as the example!

Friend, I can not remind you enough: Jesus is reality! The world's reality is ruled and dominated by death. The sinner is under the control of Satan; but thank God, Jesus took the keys over him who had the keys of death and then delivered us from him!

Hebrews 2:14-15 NLT
14 Because God's children are human beings—made of flesh and blood—the Son also became flesh and blood. For only as a human being could he die, and only by dying could he break the power of the devil, who had the power of death. 15 Only in this way could he set free all who have lived their lives as slaves to the fear of dying.

Friend, you are no longer a slave. Jesus set us free from living our lives as a slave to the fear of dying! This is the real issue on the earth and why I wanted to devote a chapter to this subject; by no means is this an exhaustive study on the subject, but I want you to get a glimpse of what Jesus provided for you in this alternate reality.

People aren't really afraid of cancer or a virus; they are afraid of dying. When you are reacting in fear, you react like the world and live like the world. Even in the middle of a plague, when you know that YOU ARE IN CONTROL OF YOUR LIFE, why is there any reason to fear? Fear is totally annihilated in your life when you know that no person and no disease can take your life.

As long as I obey what God has called me to do and follow the leading of the Holy Spirit, no one and no thing can touch me. I will choose when I am ready to leave this Earth. I will leave when (1) I have fulfilled what God has called me to do and (2) when I am satisfied and ready to go.

I will not be dominated by the curse and neither should you because Jesus has provided life far beyond what we have dreamt was possible. Live free from the fear of death because you are in control.

This is the life we get to live on the Earth. We live until we are satisfied; not until we have a disease. This is a major part of Heaven's reality: you get to walk through the valley of the shadow of death like a boss!

16

PROVISION AND PROTECTION

In the world we live in, it is filled with chaos and destruction. Fear is running rampant among people as they look to the government for financial provision as well protection from disease, crime and many other problems. Now for the sinner, I don't blame them; they understand they can't do it by themselves, so they are rightfully looking for help.

If the modern Church was actually doing its job in manifesting Heaven, the world would be looking to the Church instead of the government - but that is another subject that would take another book to deal with!

The sinner has been brought up in the world and thus, learned the world's ways and has the world's perspective. Whether people realize it or not, everyone is looking for a caretaker; the problem is the people and organizations they are looking to can't solve their problems.

Now there are certainly good-hearted, well-meaning people in this world that are not Christians. There are sinners that love people and want to do good. I recognize that and personally know some of them. However, there are problems in this world that no human being can solve or eradicate with natural ability and natural wisdom. There are some problems in this world's reality that are unchangeable by natural means.

However, in this alternate reality, we have the ultimate Caretaker! We have Someone who has not only promised, but paved the way and put us in a position to live in the world's reality but live from Heaven's reality and experience Heaven on Earth.

> Psalm 23 NLT
> 1
> The Lord is my shepherd;
>   I have all that I need.
> 2
> He lets me rest in green meadows;
>   he leads me beside peaceful streams.
> 3
>   He renews my strength.
> He guides me along right paths,
>   bringing honor to his name.
> 4
> Even when I walk
>   through the darkest valley,
> I will not be afraid,
>   for you are close beside me.
> Your rod and your staff
>   protect and comfort me.
> 5
> You prepare a feast for me

in the presence of my enemies.
You honor me by anointing my head with oil.
My cup overflows with blessings.
6
Surely your goodness and unfailing love will pursue me
all the days of my life,
and I will live in the house of the Lord
Forever.

Have you ever just stopped and read through Psalm 23? It's one of the most well known and quoted passages in the Bible. This was a reality for the psalmist under the Old Covenant; how much more so a reality for those of us that are redeemed?

"The Lord is my shepherd; I have all that I need."

Isn't that a wonderful place to be in life? Because Jesus is my shepherd, my caretaker, I have no needs, cares or worries. Friend, that right there is provision and protection!

The life Jesus will lead us through is a life of peace and rest. Yes, we may have to go through some dark valleys, but that doesn't mean the circumstances of the valley have to affect us. When we go through the valleys, we just slay some devils! We may be in this world, but we are not of it. We may be living in this world's reality, but we are living from Heaven's reality and dominating the Earth!

Look at verse 4. "Even when I walk through the darkest valley, I will not be afraid, for You are close beside me. Your rod and staff protect and comfort me." Friend, why do we worry about our life? You can't change anything with fear and worry; the only thing it does is change you.

Hebrews 13:5-6 AMP

5 Let your character [your moral essence, your inner nature] be free from the love of money [shun greed—be financially ethical], being content with what you have; for He has said, "I will never [under any circumstances] desert you [nor give you up nor leave you without support, nor will I in any degree leave you helpless], nor will I forsake or let you down or relax My hold on you [assuredly not]!" 6 So we take comfort and are encouraged and confidently say, "The Lord is my Helper [in time of need], I will not be afraid. What will man do to me?"

If you are living in fear, you are in sin and living like a sinner. Get back into faith and live like a son of God! What is there to worry about in life when Jesus has promised to never leave you or forsaken you?

THE ROD AND STAFF

In Psalms 23, the psalmist makes this wonderful statement, "Your rod and staff protect and comfort me."

So many ignorant people think God sits up in Heaven ready to beat you with a rod when you mess up. Friend, that rod isn't for you; that rod is for your enemies! The shepherd watches over the sheep with that rod to beat the mess out of any enemy that may try to attack. Jesus and your angels are there with you to protect you of any disease, any natural disaster or any person that may try to harm you.

Not only is the rod available to beat the enemy, His staff is there to protect you from getting into danger. The shepherd has his staff available to wrangle in that sheep that's trying to get off into trouble.

I don't know about you, but I have made some dumb decisions in life. In all of those dumb decisions, the Holy Spirit was right there the whole time, prompting me to change course. Now God can't over ride my will; He will let me choose stupid if I want to because He has given us a free will - a boy oh boy...when I chose stupid, I went all out!

If I would have listened though, He was trying to protect me. If we will simply listen to and be led by the Holy Spirit, even though we are walking through tough times on the Earth, He will keep me from making bad decisions like the sinner. If we will allow it, His staff can comfort us!

A FEAST OF PROVISION

The psalmist goes on to say, "You prepare a feast for me in the presence of my enemies. You honor me by anointing my head with oil. My cup overflows with blessings."

This right here is a wonderful glimpse into this alternate reality. Enemies all around you. Destruction all around you. A pandemic taking over the world. Even in the midst of chaos, God has provision for you which you didn't even have to prepare! That is just how good God is to His children.

Notice this isn't just a snack; God wants to prosper you in an amazing way when all the world is hurting and crying out for help. Why? God wants the world to see how good it is to be His kid! It is an amazing thing to look at the fear of the world and be living in the amazing and abundant provision of God - at peace with no needs or wants. Heaven's reality is a realm of life, health, provision and protection.

If Psalm 23 isn't enough, let's take a look at one of my other favorite psalms: Psalm 91.

Psalm 91 TPT
1 When you sit enthroned under the shadow of Shaddai, you are hidden in the strength of God Most High.
2 He's the hope that holds me and the Stronghold to shelter me, the only God for me, and my great confidence.
3 He will rescue you from every hidden trap of the enemy, and he will protect you from false accusation
and any deadly curse
4 His massive arms are wrapped around you, protecting you. You can run under his covering of majesty and hide. His arms of faithfulness are a shield keeping you from harm.
5 You will never worry about an attack of demonic forces at night nor have to fear a spirit of darkness coming against you.
6 Don't fear a thing! Whether by night or by day, demonic danger will not trouble you, nor will the powers of evil launched against you.
7 Even in a time of disaster, with thousands and thousands being killed, you will remain unscathed and unharmed.
8 you will be a spectator as the wicked perish in judgment, for they will be paid back for what they have done!
9–10 When we live our lives within the shadow of God Most High, our secret hiding place, we will always be shielded from harm.
How then could evil prevail against us or disease infect

us?

11 God sends angels with special orders to protect you wherever you go, defending you from all harm.

12 If you walk into a trap, they'll be there for you and keep you from stumbling.

13 You'll even walk unharmed among the fiercest powers of darkness, trampling every one of them beneath your feet!

14 For here is what the Lord has spoken to me: "Because you have delighted in me as my great lover, I will greatly protect you. I will set you in a high place, safe and secure before my face.

15 I will answer your cry for help every time you pray, and you will find and feel my presence even in your time of pressure and trouble. I will be your glorious hero and give you a feast.

16 You will be satisfied with a full life and with all that I do for you. For you will enjoy the fullness of my salvation!"

If reading Psalm 91 doesn't make you feel almost invincible, I don't know what will. It is one of the most amazing promises in the Bible regarding God's provision and protection - and it is for us today!

ABIDE IN HIM

In verse one, God tells us that if we will make Him our dwelling place, all of these things will happen for us. To *dwell* simply means to "abide or stay put." In other words, if we will maintain our consciousness of God in us and maintain the perspective of Heaven, protection and provision are ours. You can't put your faith on something you are not aware of; it is just that simple and yet, it is the reason so many people quote scriptures but experience Hell on Earth. You can make declarations of faith, bind the devil, quote scriptures and go through all the motions Christians do, but if you are more conscious of the problem than the Provider, your motions will only create wind.

Jesus referred to this in John 15:5.

> John 15:5 NKJV
> I am the vine, you are the branches. He who abides in Me, and I in him, bears much fruit; for without Me you can do nothing.

Dwelling or abiding has much to do with your consciousness and awareness of God. What your mind is on is what will be your reality. If your perspective is that of the world's reality, then you will experience the realm of death even though Jesus transferred you into the realm of life. This is why Christians today do not experience victory. Instead of abiding in Christ where victory is already had, most of us abide in the world where victory needs to be obtained.

> ***What your mind is on is what will be your reality.***

Psalm 91 is an outright declaration of God's protection and provision for us despite the death around us. If there ever was a time for the Church to grab hold of this wonderful reality, it is now. Never on planet Earth has there ever been a more dangerous and destructive time and yet, it is only going to get worse. There are diseases coming down the pipeline of Hell that will ravage countries and despite the advances of medicine, there will be no medicines that will solve it. There will be violence and destruction like has never been seen and it will only be the hand of the Lord upon His people that will protect them.

A SHIELD OF PROTECTION

I believe we are coming into a day in which we will see once again something similar to what happened with Moses and the Israelites in the land of Goshen. The plagues were affecting the Egyptians but were not affecting the Israelites. Even when the Egyptians were experiencing total darkness, the Israelites had daylight. The Israelites had a supernatural shield around them protecting them from the plagues!

The same thing is not just a promise to us but a reality for us in this alternate reality. When we make the decision to not just be saved in word only, but abide in that salvation, we will experience provision and protection beyond what we have dreamed possible.

> Psalm 91:10,14 TPT
> "When we live our lives within the shadow of God Most High, our secret hiding place, we will always be shielded from harm. How then could evil prevail against us or disease infect us? I will greatly protect you. I will set you in a high place, safe and secure before my face."

No government can do this for you. No hospital can do this for you. No insurance can do this for you. No one can provide and protect you like God! Let's move on from just singing songs and quoting Scriptures that we don't believe. Let's get to the place in our soul where we know these things to be true! This isn't a time to play games anymore; no more playing Christian. *Jesus has paid too high of a price for us to go through life on the Earth and continue experiencing the death realm we were delivered from.*

Heaven isn't denying there are problems on the earth, but Heaven does see that we can walk right through the fire and not even smell like smoke.

> Daniel 3:16-27 NLT
> 16 Shadrach, Meshach, and Abednego replied, "O Nebuchadnezzar, we do not need to defend ourselves before you. 17 If we are thrown into the blazing furnace, the God whom we serve is able to save us. He will rescue us from your power, Your Majesty. 18 But even if he doesn't, we want to make it clear to you, Your Majesty, that we will never serve your gods or worship the gold statue you have set up." 19 Nebuchadnezzar was so furious with Shadrach, Meshach, and Abednego that his face became distorted with rage. He commanded that the furnace be heated seven times hotter than usual. 20 Then he ordered some of the strongest men of his army to bind Shadrach, Meshach, and Abednego and throw them into the blazing furnace. 21 So they tied them up and threw them into the furnace, fully dressed in their pants, turbans, robes, and other garments. 22 And because the king, in his anger, had demanded such a hot fire in the furnace, the flames killed the soldiers as they threw the three men in. 23 So Shadrach, Meshach, and Abednego, securely tied, fell into the roaring flames. 24 But suddenly, Nebuchadnezzar jumped up in amazement and exclaimed to his advisers, "Didn't we tie up three men and throw them into the furnace?" "Yes, Your Majesty, we certainly did," they replied. 25 "Look!" Nebuchadnezzar shouted. "I see four men, unbound, walking around in the fire

unharmed! And the fourth looks like a god " 26 Then Nebuchadnezzar came as close as he could to the door of the flaming furnace and shouted: "Shadrach, Meshach, and Abednego, servants of the Most High God, come out! Come here!" So Shadrach, Meshach, and Abednego stepped out of the fire. 27 Then the high officers, officials, governors, and advisers crowded around them and saw that the fire had not touched them. Not a hair on their heads was singed, and their clothing was not scorched. They didn't even smell of smoke!

The story of Shadrach, Meshach and Abednego is a powerful example of provision and protection in this alternate reality. Because they refused to bow down to the king, they were thrown into the blazing furnace. The furnace was so hot the fire killed the soldiers who threw the three men into it! However, Shadrach, Meshach and Abednego were just fine. King Nebuchadnezzar saw the three men walking around in the fire and talking to a fourth man.

When the king brought Shadrach, Meshach and Abednego out, their hair, skin, clothes - nothing was touched by the fire! They were in the fire but the fire wasn't in them. *They were literally living in the curse but living from the Blessing!* God's life was so much in force that the three men usurped physical law.

How did this happen? The three men made a decision to make God their dwelling. Because they chose to put their trust in God, *they literally stepped over into another reality all the while their physical bodies being in the same place.* They were physically in the same place as everyone else but having a different experience! Why? An alternate reality; Heaven's reality while on Earth!

17

A LIFESTYLE OF MIRACLES

In the reality of Heaven, miracles are just normal. In one sense, there isn't anything spectacular about the things of God because it's just normal in this alternate reality. Miracles are simply God invading this realm and acting normal. Miracles are signs for the unbeliever, but simply a way of life for the person united with Christ.

John 5:20 NKJV
For the Father loves the Son, and shows Him all things that He Himself does; and He will show Him greater works than these, that you may marvel.

The reason we are so amazed when we see miracles is because our mind isn't fully renewed to the things of God. Now I'm certainly not discounting our amazement and wonder at the awesomeness of God. At this point in my life and ministry, I have lost count at the number of blind and deaf we have seen healed. To watch someone regain their sight is awesome and the power of God always amazes me - but there is a major difference in being in awe of God and in awe of the miracle.

> *Many of us are carrying the rod of anointing but asking Pharoah for help.*

When we are in awe of the miracle, it simply reveals we still have some cursed thinking we need to deal with. Let's just get real here: it should not surprise us to see a missing limb grow out or to see a child with down syndrome instantly healed before our eyes.

These things are supposed to happen - do you know why? Because God sent us to invade this world's reality and manifest His reality. We are God's agents of change. We are the carriers of His anointing and life!

Due to cursed thinking, we still have the perspective of the world even though we have the equipment of God and the position of God on the Earth. Now I know that last part may have caused you to do a double take but it is the truth. Just as God made Moses "as God to Pharaoh," He has made us as God to Satan.

> Exodus 7:1 NKJV
> So the Lord said to Moses: "See, I have made you as God to Pharaoh, and Aaron your brother shall be your prophet."

After the cross, Jesus defeated Satan, stripped him of his authority over us and then united us with the Father, the Son and the Holy Spirit. Jesus sent us into the world to continue His ministry of setting the captives free; the problem is many of us are carrying the rod of anointing but asking Pharaoh for help.

WHY ARE WE LOOKING TO THE WORLD TO DELIVER US?

We are looking to the world to deliver us from the world's problems. Why? Because we either do not know or have forgotten that God has given us everything we need in this life to live like Heaven on Earth.

2 Peter 1:3-4 AMPC
3 For His divine power has bestowed upon us all things that [are requisite and suited] to life and godliness, through the full, personal] knowledge of Him Who called us by and to His own glory and excellence (virtue). 4 By means of these He has bestowed on us His precious and exceedingly great promises, so that through them you may escape [by flight] from the moral decay (rottenness and corruption) that is in the world because of covetousness (lust and greed), and become sharers (partakers) of the divine nature.

2 Peter 1:3-4 NLT
3 By his divine power, God has given us everything we need for living a godly life. We have received all of this by coming to know him, the one who called us to himself by means of his marvelous glory and excellence. 4 And because of his glory and excellence, he has given us great and precious promises. These are the promises that enable you to share his divine nature and escape the world's corruption caused by human desires.

2 Peter 1:4 TPT
...so that through the power of these tremendous promises you can experience partnership with the divine nature...

God has given us everything we need to live a godly life; not just a life full of godly behaviors, but a godly life full of dominion...life as God would live! These powerful promises enable us to escape the corruption in this world. By becoming sharers of His divine nature, it allows us to live above the sin, sickness, and poverty in this world. Through our union with Him, we can live in this world, but not live from it!

Just as God sent Jesus, Jesus has sent us (John 17:18) and yet, just as Jesus spent time with the Father, we need to do so as well. Jesus said the Father would show Him even greater things than what He had seen up until that point. Our fellowship with the Father will help remove the "wow" factor in our life. Again, I'm not saying we stop marveling at the goodness of God; I am saying we need to get to the point of seeing that (1) anything is possible with God on this Earth and (2) He can use me to do it.

You will never find promises of God and realities of Heaven that limit you as to what you can do for Him. All the realities of our union with Christ actually do the opposite: *they take off the limits!* You will find there is not an equipment problem when it comes to representing Heaven; there is only an awareness problem of knowing what we have and Who is with us.

In Heaven's reality, miracles are normal and we are the agents in which God is endeavoring to use to make the world marvel and open their hearts unto Him.

18

ALWAYS ON OFFENSE

One of the major reasons we do not see the results in the miraculous as Jesus did is because we do not respond as Jesus did. You will find Jesus did not react to negative situations; Jesus responded to negative situations. When problems arose, Jesus did not react in fear; He responded in faith.

Luke 8:22-25 NKJV
22 Now it happened, on a certain day, that He got into a boat with His disciples. And He said to them, "Let us cross over to the other side of the lake." And they launched out. 23 But as they sailed He fell asleep. And a windstorm came down on the lake, and they were filling with water, and were in jeopardy. 24 And they came to Him and awoke Him, saying, "Master, Master, we are perishing!"Then He arose and rebuked the wind and the raging of the water. And they ceased, and there was a calm. 25 But He said to them, "Where is your faith?" And they were afraid, and marveled, saying to one another, "Who can this be? For He commands even the

winds and water, and they obey Him!"

When the disciples became afraid of the storm, they reacted in fear; they suddenly were on defense. Jesus didn't react as they did; Jesus simply responded in faith with His authority and said to the storm, "Shhhh." Jesus' response was calm, cool and collected!

WHOEVER HAS THE BALL HAS CONTROL

You will find that Jesus was always on offense; He wasn't reactionary to the situations because Jesus knew He was in control of the ball.

In most sports involving a ball, you have an offense and a defense. When you are on defense, your object is to get the ball and your actions are almost always reactionary. Sure, there are plays you run on defense to try and make the offense go where you want to, but you are still in a position of reacting to what the offense does.

On offense, you have the ball and you are in control and in many ways, it's a lot easier on offense than it is on defense. I grew up playing basketball and was a very good shooter, but I loved playing defense. I loved going after the best player and just flat out shutting them down with my hustle and tenacity; however, I expended much more energy on defense than I did on offense.

On offense, we could simply pass the ball around and make the defense chase it; this was especially the case when the defense wanted to run a trap. It didn't bother me at all as long as you stayed calm and kept your composure and understood: you are in control of this situation. The whole purpose of the defense running their trap was to go really quick and get you to react with a dumb decision.

This is exactly what Satan tries to do on the earth. Most Christians do not know it, but the moment they are saved, they are put on offense with the ball in their hand. The power becomes theirs, the authority becomes theirs and the position becomes theirs. However, if you don't know you have the ball, you will think you are on defense trying to get the ball. This is why most Christians act the way they do and pray the way they do!

In Heaven's reality, we are always on offense, but if you don't know it, you'll act like cursed people trying to get their victory.

Colossians 2:15 AMP
When He had disarmed the rulers and authorities [those supernatural forces of evil operating against us], He made a public example of them [exhibiting them as captives in His triumphal procession], having triumphed over them through the cross.

Colossians 2:15 TPT
Then Jesus made a public spectacle of all the powers and principalities of darkness, stripping away from them every weapon and all their spiritual authority and power to accuse us. And by the power of the cross, Jesus led them around as prisoners in a procession of triumph. He was not their prisoner; they were his!

Do you see it? Jesus not only defeated Satan once and for all, but He stripped Satan of all his authority over us. Because of what Jesus did, we are on offense...forever!

Not only that, but check this out: because Satan has no authority over you, he can't even take the ball away from you. The only way he can get the ball is if you give it to him.

> Genesis 3:1-7 NLT
> 1 The serpent was the shrewdest of all the wild animals the Lord God had made. One day he asked the woman, "Did God really say you must not eat the fruit from any of the trees in the garden?" 2 "Of course we may eat fruit from the trees in the garden," the woman replied. 3 "It's only the fruit from the tree in the middle of the garden that we are not allowed to eat. God said, 'You must not eat it or even touch it; if you do, you will die.'" 4 "You won't die!" the serpent replied to the woman. 5 "God knows that your eyes will be opened as soon as you eat it, and you will be like God, knowing both good and evil." 6 The woman was convinced. She saw that the tree was beautiful and its fruit looked delicious, and she wanted the wisdom it would give her. So she took some of the fruit and ate it. Then she gave some to her husband, who was with her, and he ate it, too. 7 At that moment their eyes were opened, and they suddenly felt shame at their nakedness. So they sewed fig leaves together to cover themselves.

Before the curse came into play, Satan was in the very same position with God's people; Satan had no authority and couldn't do anything but what God's people would allow. Satan used to have the authority Adam and Eve had and wanted it back, but he couldn't just take it.

Satan deceived Eve with a lie. Satan told Eve that if she would eat of the fruit, she would become like God. What was the deception? Eve was already like God but she didn't know it. Satan was wanting

Eve to try and get the ball when she actually already had the ball in her hand - she just didn't know it!

YOU ARE NOT TRYING TO GET THE BALL

It is actually the same today because of redemption. Jesus translated us into the kingdom of Heaven; righteousness, prosperity, forgiveness, safety and healing are already ours...BUT, if you don't know it, you will always be trying to get it. You will think you are on defense trying to get the ball.

Your prayers will be spent on begging God to give you what He already gave you! Your confessions will come not from a perspective of "I have it," but from a perspective of "I need it." *Much of our prayer and confession is coming from a place of fear and not of faith and that is why good hearted God loving people die on their deathbed quoting healing scriptures.*

We must see from Heaven's perspective! We must see ourselves from the place of victory. Righteous people aren't trying to get forgiven. Healed people aren't trying to get healed.

Now, if there is a situation in which we have dropped our guard and we sinned, we don't try to get forgiven - we simply receive the forgiveness already provided.

If there is a situation in which we have dropped our guard and sickness has come, we don't try to get healed - we simply receive the healing already provided.

Friend, we have to stop giving Satan authority he doesn't have.

In many ways, Satan is a non-issue. Yes, we have an enemy that is roaming around seeking whom he can devour, but that is the key: he is looking for who he CAN devour.

> 1 Peter 5:8 NLT
> Stay alert! Watch out for your great enemy, the devil. He prowls around like a roaring lion, looking for someone to devour.

SATAN NEEDS YOUR AUTHORITY

In other words, just as with Eve, Satan can't do anything unless we give him permission. Yes, we stay on guard and do as God told Adam because Satan is always trying to take the ball - but he can not take it unless you give it to him.

If we made a mistake and gave him the ball, do you know what we do? We demand Satan to let go and he will. Satan doesn't have a choice in the matter because he has no authority over us. When we were redeemed, we went from being Satan's slaves to being Satan's master!

This is why, when we are in a situation that needs a touch of Heaven, we don't cry and moan, complain and grumble; we don't start begging God and going through all of the rituals that many Christians do. Our response is like that of Jesus: someone who is in absolute control of the situation.

> Acts 20:1-12 AMP
> 1 Now on the first day of the week (Sunday), when we were gathered together to break bread (share communion), Paul began talking with them, intending to leave the next

day; and he kept on with his message until midnight. 8 Now there were many lamps in the upper room where we were assembled, 9 and there was a young man named Eutychus ("Lucky") sitting on the window sill. He was sinking into a deep sleep, and as Paul kept on talking longer and longer, he was completely overcome by sleep and fell down from the third story; and he was picked up dead. 10 But Paul went down and threw himself on him and embraced him, and said [to those standing around him], "Do not be troubled, because he is alive." 11 When Paul had gone back upstairs and had broken the bread and eaten, he talked [informally and confidentially] with them for a long time—until daybreak [in fact]—and then he left. 12 They took the boy [Eutychus] home alive, and were greatly comforted and encouraged.

People falling asleep in church has been going on since the beginning! I would say that Eutychus probably had more of an excuse than some of us; Paul had already been teaching until midnight! Eutychus fell asleep and fell three stories to the ground and died on impact.

What was Paul's response? It wasn't a prayer meeting to try and bring Eutychus back from the dead! Paul knew his authority and that he possessed the life of God. Paul went down to Eutychus' body, laid on top of him, released the life of God and stated, "Do not be troubled; he is alive."

After Eutychus was raised from the dead in the early hour of the morning, everyone went upstairs, ate a meal and then Paul kept on teaching until sunrise!

We must know the control that is ours in this alternate reality. We are in control. I know people like to say God is in control but actually, He only has as much control in your life as you allow. You are the prophet of your life. What you say is what will come to pass. What you allow is what will be allowed.

> Matthew 16:19 NKJV
> And I will give you the keys of the kingdom of heaven, and whatever you bind on earth will be bound in heaven, and whatever you loose on earth will be loosed in heaven."

We are in control of manifesting Heaven's reality in the cursed reality of the world. We are not trying to get the keys; we have the keys! When I have the key to a door, I choose when I want to open it and when I want to lock it. Do you see it? Through redemption, God put us on offense; He gave us back control of our lives. Before we were slaves with no say so; now, we have a say so and we must start saying so!

When you begin to see the position you are in, it will make it so very easy for us when it comes time to dealing with the attacks of Satan. Yes, he will bring attacks and yes, we should be watching; yet, all Satan can do is bring lying thoughts and deceptions in this sense realm to try and get you to let go of the ball.

SOUL CONTROL

Every miracle Jesus performed, He was in control. He was not only in control of the situation, but He was also in control of His soul. Friend, if you don't keep your emotions and thoughts in control during the storms of life, you will drown while you make faith declarations. Although God has put you in control and given you the keys, you will never experience the victory Jesus provided until you first control your soul.

The power of God is magnificent! The power of God can wipe out a cancer but it can't wipe out your cares. You are the one in control of your soul. Jesus saved your spirit but you have the responsibility of saving your soul by the renewing of your mind. Again, too many Christians are praying from a perspective of fear and defeat.

When you do this, you are already on the losing side. This is why we see so many people start calling everyone they know to pray when a negative situation arises. Now again, the prayer of agreement is scriptural and I am certainly for groups praying in regards to a situation...BUT, how many times do you see Jesus call for group prayer about a situation?

> *The power of God can wipe out a cancer but it can't wipe out your cares.*

When the storms of life arose, Jesus arose and handled it. When our first response is to start calling people and send out social media blasts, could it be we have more faith in other people's connection to God than our own? Could it be we don't believe we are actually holding the keys to the Kingdom?

If you are on defense, it is time to change sides. Stop acting like the world and most of the Church; let us start acting like Jesus. You are always a winner going somewhere to win! You are more than a conqueror! You are always on offense! See yourself from Heaven's perspective: victorious and always in control.

19

PEACE AND PRESENCE

The world's reality is one dominated by stress which has its roots in fear. All of Satan's tactics are zeroed in on one thing: your peace. Satan knows that if he can take your peace, he has taken you out.

Stress has become such a common force in the world that people have accepted it even though they know it is killing them. Much research has been in this area which has proven the affects stress has on the human body.

Both Japan and Korea recognize suicide as an official and compensatable work-related condition due to stress and being overworked. The estimated prevalence of stress and stress-related conditions in the United Kingdom rose from 829 cases per 100,000 workers in 1990 to 1,700 per 100,000 in 2001/2002. In that year, 13.4 million lost working days were attributed to stress, anxiety or depression, with an estimate 265,000 new cases of stress. It is estimated that 80% to 90% of all industrial accidents are related to personal problem and employees' inability to handle stress. The European Agency for Safety and Health at work reported that about 50% of job absenteeism is caused by stress.

The morbidity and mortality due to stress-related illness is alarming. Emotional stress is a major contributing factor to the six leading causes of death in the United States: cancer, coronary heart disease, accidental injuries, respiratory disorders, cirrhosis of the liver and suicide. According to statistics from Meridian Stress Management Consultancy in the U.K, almost 180,000 people in the U.K die each year from some form of stress-related illness. The Centre for Disease Control and Prevention of the United States estimates that stress account about 75% of all doctors visit. This involves an extremely wide span of physical complaints including, but not limited to headache, back pain, heart problems, upset stomach, stomach ulcer, sleep problems, tiredness and accidents. According to Occupational Health and Safety news and the National Council on compensation of insurance, up to 90% of all visits to primary care physicians are for stress-related complaints. (Stress and Illness; Malays J Med Sci. 2008 Oct).

In a day and time in which technology has advanced like none other, we have scores of appliances, tools, gadgets and software to help us have it easier in life. Instead of bringing peace to our life, our drive has allowed technology to be an enemy of our peace by making us do even more. Instead of getting a job done faster, the focus is on getting more jobs done in the same amount of time.

Productivity is wonderful, but not at the cost of peace.

If it is not job related stress, there are always more to choose from: financial, relational, physical and familial. You can always add more onto that too! In the world, there is an assortment of areas to choose from and *Satan will make sure they never run out.*

In this world's reality, peace is the absence of a problem; therefore, there is always a push to get rid of that problem. But the problem is, more stress comes from trying to get rid of the problem causing the initial stress! The sinner can try as hard as they want, but they will never experience true peace. You

> *Peace isn't the absence of something; it's the Presence of Someone.*

can try and remove all of the anxiety filled issues in life by lighting a candle, meditating and playing your Zen music, but as soon as another problem arises, your candle and music won't change anything.

In Heaven's reality, peace is the dominating force; it's the air we breathe and yet it is a Person. In Heaven's reality, peace isn't the absence of something; it is the presence of Someone.

In Jesus' last hours with the disciples before going to the cross, Jesus makes a powerful statement and gives a tremendous gift.

> John 14:27 NKJV
> Peace I leave with you, My peace I give to you; not as the world gives do I give to you. Let not your heart be troubled, neither let it be afraid.

If Jesus is telling you not to let your heart be troubled or be afraid, it is because (1) you have a choice and (2) He knows it will harm and hinder you.

In Heaven's reality, peace isn't something I'm searching for; peace is something I have. I hope you have noticed this major difference in this alternate reality; the things the world is searching for are the things we already have. Our union with Christ provided everything we would ever need on the Earth and the most valuable asset we have is peace.

Friend, this last year I have watched people all over the world live in constant panic over the covid 19 virus. The stress and fear of it has made some people act a little crazy! I actually have a neighbor that hasn't left their house in nine months because they are deathly afraid of this virus! While this virus has gone around the world, and sadly has killed some people, I have lived care free throughout it all. Why would I worry about a virus when I have His presence?

DENIAL

In Heaven's reality, I am not denying the problem; I am denying its influence in my life. Notice Jesus didn't tell the disciples He was removing all of the problems of the world. He didn't promise a life free of issues; He promised a life of peace while dominating the issues.

I will not allow cursed things to influence me. In this world, I am the change agent; not the one to be changed. How does this happen though? How can we be in the middle of a pandemic and yet not respond like everyone else?

Philippians 4:6-7 NLT
6 Don't worry about anything; instead, pray about everything. Tell God what you need, and thank him for all he has done. 7 Then you will experience God's peace, which exceeds anything we can understand. His peace will guard your hearts and minds as you live in Christ Jesus.

PROTECT YOUR PEACE

God has given us instructions that if we will protect our peace, He will protect us. When I choose to guard what I have, He will guard me. Friend, I'm not looking for peace; I am protecting my peace.

At this stage of my life, I have determined that peace in my life is not optional. No matter what happens, no matter what comes my way, I refuse to give my peace up. It truly has become something that is at the forefront of my mind: protecting and maintaining my peace.

If I do not protect my peace, it will ruin me in a number of ways. Not only will it affect my body, it will also affect my influence in the world. Remember, we are the change agents because we are not only sent from Heaven, but we are a carriers of Him. If I react to a situation in fear just like the sinner, I have removed my ability to manifest Heaven. Without peace, I can no longer manifest the anointing because my soul has been consumed with the problem. I can no longer be a change agent when I have been changed.

Jesus always responded from Presence - never reacting from

fear. Heaven's response is different than the world's reaction: peace flows from Heaven; fear flows from the world.

In the midst of a pandemic, I must protect my peace. I can not allow myself to see from the perspective of the cursed world; otherwise, despite being a carrier of God, I will have the same experience as the world. If I am having the same experience, how can I show them the Way? If I have given up my peace, how can I give that individual peace?

Not only will a lack of peace affect my influence, it will also affect my consciousness of God - and that my friend is number one on my list. Why? Because without a consciousness of God, I am no good in the world. I may be able to quote scriptures and sound smart, but without being aware of Him, I have become a lecturer instead of a deliverer.

It is peace that enables me to fulfill the plan of God for my life. How can I be led by the Holy Spirit if I am more conscious of the negative situation than Him? I am to say what I hear Him say and do what I see Him do - but that isn't possible when fear and stress is dominating me.

NO PEACE, NO CONNECTION

No peace means no connection. No connection with the power and no connection with Him. Certainly, I can do nothing about my position with God - nothing can change that. However, me protecting my peace has everything to do with my connection or fellowship with God. There are many voices in this world and they are consumed with fear, anxiety and stress. The more voices that I allow in my life, the harder it will be for me to hear from Him. My soul must be absent of those voices and totally consumed with His voice - the only way that happens is by protecting my peace.

LIVING CAREFREE

I made the decision several years ago that come what may, I refuse to allow stress in my life; I just won't do it. I've been accused by those around me for "not caring" when it comes to problems. They are correct because I refuse to take on the cares of this world.

I have had people actually get really mad at me because I wouldn't "pet" their cares. I am very black and white when it comes to life; I just don't see much gray. They are consumed with care and want me to feel with them. Yes, I have compassion on people and their situation, but my job isn't to agree with you on how bad it is; my job is to help you see how things really are in this alternate reality.

If I am consumed with emotion, I am probably consumed with care. If I am consumed with the care, then I am not consumed with Him. My job is to cast the care over on God and let Him take care of it!

If the washer breaks, well, we just go buy another one. If a bill comes due in which there isn't money for, well, God will provide it. If the house burns down, well, we have insurance...we just get another one. There are so many things in this world that in some ways, you can't do anything about - so why worry about them? Worry has never changed a situation, but it will always change you!

Matthew 6:25-34 NLT

25 "That is why I tell you not to worry about everyday life—whether you have enough food and drink, or enough clothes to wear. Isn't life more than food, and your body more than clothing? 26 Look at the birds. They don't plant or harvest or store food in barns, for your heavenly Father feeds them. And aren't you far more valuable to him than they are? 27 Can all your worries add a single moment to your life? 28 "And why worry about your clothing? Look at the lilies of the field and how they grow. They don't work or make their clothing, 29 yet Solomon in all his glory was not dressed as beautifully as they are. 30 And if God cares so wonderfully for wildflowers that are here today and thrown into the fire tomorrow, he will certainly care for you. Why do you have so little faith? 31 "So don't worry about these things, saying, 'What will we eat? What will we drink? What will we wear?' 32 These things dominate the thoughts of unbelievers, but your heavenly Father already knows all your needs. 33 Seek the Kingdom of God above all else, and live righteously, and he will give you everything you need. 34 "So don't worry about tomorrow, for tomorrow will bring its own worries. Today's trouble is enough for today.

In Heaven's reality, everything has already been provided because God is our Provider. Why worry? The only reason we worry is because we think we have to get it. Maybe it's more serious than a broken washer; maybe it is a bad medical report. Ok - so what?

Believe me, I understand. Hearing from the doctor that you have a cancerous tumor in your body...it can be a tremendous shock to your soul if you aren't staying grounded in Christ. However, when you know Jesus is the Healer, that healing has not only been promised, but a reality for us - what is there to worry about?

The reason we worry when it comes to healing is because we've been religiously brainwashed and we got it from the world's reality. We think we have to get it. Friend, if you think you have to get it, it's because you are seeing like a cursed person instead of a blessed person. You don't have to try and obtain what has already been put in your spirit. As people of Heaven, we don't obtain; we protect. We protect because Christ has already obtained the victory and made available all the resources of Heaven (Ephesians 1:3).

NECESSARY TO WIN

People filled with worry have let go of their peace. Refuse to be moved from the position of peace. You should treat it like the air you breathe: absolutely necessary for life. I must realize that if I am not at peace, I am not winning. I have let my guard down and invited Satan to have his way.

Remember, Satan has no authority in my life; the only way he can do anything is if I allow it. One way I give him authority is when I give him my peace. If you have let go of your peace, allowed your heart to become troubled and gotten into fear - what do you do? Repent. Change your direction! The moment you repent, you immediately get it back. Protect your peace at all costs. No peace - no faith - no victory.

Jesus is the Way, the Truth and the Life. He is the Way to what is reality - a reality filled and consumed with the life of God. If

213

He is peace, there is no other way to access and walk in all He has available for me. Protect your peace and you protect the anointing. Protect your peace and you protect your connection. Protect your peace and He will protect you.

Friend, protect your peace and you will experience Heaven on Earth and reveal to the world Heaven's normal way of living.

ABOUT THE AUTHOR

Chad and Lacy Gonzales are graduates of Rhema Bible Training College. Chad holds an M.Ed. in Counseling from Lamar University and a D.Min. from School of Bible Theology and Seminary.

With an emphasis on healing and one's union with Christ, Chad brings a powerful and practical message of faith and grace. The mission of Chad Gonzales Ministries is to connect people to God so they can manifest God to their world.

Declaring the Gospel with simplicity, boldness and humor, mighty miracles of healing are normal in their meetings.

Together with their son Jake, they minister around the world teaching and proving that Jesus is THE WAY.

OTHER BOOKS AVAILABLE

Aliens

Believing God For A House

Eight Percent

Fearless

God's Will Is You Healed

Healed

Making Right Decisions

Naturally Supernatural

The Freedom Of Forgiveness

Think Like Jesus

Walking In The Miraculous

What's Next

The Supernatural Life Podcast

Check out The Supernatural Life Podcast with Chad Gonzales! New episodes are available each month designed to help you connect with God on a deeper level and live the supernatural life God desires for you to have.

The Healing Academy is an outreach of Chad Gonzales Ministries to help the everyday believer learn to walk according to the standard of Jesus in the ministry of healing.

Jesus said in John 14:12 that whoever believes in Him would do the same works and even greater works. Through The Healing Academy, it is our goal to raise the standard of the healing ministry in the Church and manifest the ministry of Jesus in the marketplace.

The Healing Academy is available by video training series as well as in person training. For more information, please visit ChadGonzales.com

Prayer For Salvation And The Baptism Of The Holy Spirit

Dear friend, it is the desire of God that everyone accepts His free gift of salvation. God sent the greatest gift Heaven had so the world could be set free; that precious gift was Jesus! Despite knowing the mistakes you would make, He died for you anyway. Jesus knew the mistakes you would make, yet He still climbed up on the cross. Why? His love was greater than your sin.

Romans 10:9-10 says if you will confess Jesus as your Lord and Savior and believe that He arose from the dead, you will be saved. You see, salvation has nothing to do with works. It doesn't matter what church you belong to, how many little old ladies you help across the street or how much you give the church. You cannot earn salvation; you cannot buy salvation; you must simply accept salvation.

Another free gift that God has provided is the Baptism of the Holy Spirit. In Acts 2, we find the Baptism of the Holy Spirit being given to the Church. God desires that you be filled with His Spirit with the evidence of speaking in tongues.

God said in Acts 2:38 that this life changing gift was for everyone, not just a select few. It wasn't just for those living in Bible days; it was given to everyone who would accept Jesus as Lord and Savior. Jesus said the purpose of the Baptism of the Holy Spirit was so you could be a witness! You'll find that when you receive the Baptism of the Holy Spirit, it allows you to operate in the fullness of God's power and be a blessing to the entire world. Essentially, you could say that salvation gets you into a relationship with God and the Baptism of the Holy Spirit helps you get others into a relationship with God.

Regardless of who you are, God has a plan for your life. He wants you to be successful, have all your needs met and live a life of victory. God wants every day of your life to be a day full of peace and joy, but it all begins with Jesus being your Lord and Savior. If you have never accepted Jesus as your Lord and Savior, please pray this prayer with me right now:

Jesus, I confess that I am a sinner. I realize I can't do this on my own. I believe with my heart and confess with my mouth that you died on the cross for my sins and sicknesses and arose from the dead. I ask you to be the Lord and Savior of my life. I thank you for forgiving me of my sins and loving me enough to give your life for me. I thank you that I am now a child of God! I now ask you for the Baptism of the Holy Spirit. You said in Your Word that it was a free gift so I receive it now. I thank you for my Heavenly prayer language!

We encourage you to become involved in a solid Bible based church. If you need help finding a church in your area, contact us through the information below.

Begin reading your Bible and praying in the Spirit daily. Now it is time to start developing your relationship with your Heavenly Father and growing in the Lord - and don't forget to tell someone about what Jesus did for you! Remember that God is good and He has good things in store for you!

If you prayed this prayer, would like assistance in locating a local church or this book has impacted your life, we would love to hear from you! You can also obtain a full listing of our books and other teaching materials by contacting us at:

www.ChadGonzales.com

Made in the USA
Las Vegas, NV
22 March 2022

46156792R00125